The Secret of Breaking The Cycle of Defeat

Tom Tirivangani

THE SECRET OF BREAKING THE CYCLE OF DEFEAT

Published by
Tom Tirivangani Press and Publications
200 Sanford Ave North, Hamilton, Ontario
Canada L8L5Z8

Copyright © 2024 by Tom Tirivangani
All rights reserved. All rights reserved.
No part of this publication may be reproduced, stored in a retrieval system, or transmitted in any form or by any means except in the case of a brief quotation printed in articles or reviews without prior permission in writing from the publisher

First Printing, 2024

Unless otherwise identified, Scripture quotations are taken from the New King James Version®. Copyright © 1982 by Thomas Nelson. Used by permission. All rights reserved.

Scripture quotations identified NIV are taken from the NEW INTERNATIONAL VERSION, Holy Bible, New International Version®, NIV® Copyright ©1973, 1978, 1984, 2011 by Biblica, Inc.® Used by permission. All rights reserved worldwide.

Scripture quotations identified AMPC are taken from the Amplified Bible, Classic Edition. Copyright © 1954, 1958, 1962, 1964, 1965, 1987 by The Lockman Foundation

Contents

1	Stepping Into the Battle	1
2	Unmasking the Deceitfulness of Failure	11
3	Your Mindset as Key	17
4	Understanding the Essence of the Battle	33
5	The Three Master Keys	49
6	The Temptation to Forget	59
7	The Power Of Character	69
8	The Hidden Mystery of Thanksgiving	79
9	The People Matrix	89
10	Prophecy as Both Knife and Medicine	99
11	Ancient Wisdom in Dealing with Difficult Battles	109
12	The Denouement	119

1

Stepping Into the Battle

"Life must be lived on principle and purpose. To do otherwise is a trap Satan has used for generations to destroy great destinies." —Prophet Tom Tirivangani

It is clear that God is a God of principle and purpose. He is a meticulous God— A master planner and executor. Just look at the cosmos and the world around you, and you will discover the complexity and meticulousness of God. God is a God of simplicity, yet complex and unique. He blends simplicity and complexity with a level of shrewdness and wisdom that defy human comprehension. Everything He does is done with such immeasurable precision and distinction, leaving no room for misalignment, failure or even confusion.

Paul exhorted the Church, saying, "Let all things be done decently and in order" (1 Cor.14.40). It is not just the decency that things are done righteously and correctly, but it is the decency of doing things in a fulfilling and orderly way. God understood that humanity could not fulfil its divine purpose for life without sufficient knowledge and understanding of what they were called to do.

The voice of God offers caution and instruction. As Hosea 4:6 declares, "My people are destroyed for lack of knowledge. Because you have rejected knowledge, I also will reject you from being priest for Me; because you have forgotten the law of your God, I also will forget your children." The trap of every man has been the lack of knowledge.

There were generations where the quest for knowledge was a quest held in high esteem. Knowledge was held as the prince and king of life. Parents would spend thousands of dollars to educate their children. People had such a deep quest for knowledge that they would not give up the search for knowledge. Many spent sleepless nights burning candles, reading books and sitting under the tutelage of those who were deemed to be knowledgeable. Teachers occupied a sacred position in society because humanity recognized that it was impossible to succeed in any field or endeavour without knowledge.

During Zimbabwe's liberation struggle, countless heroes obtained three or four diplomas while confined in prison. The prison could not confine and quench their thirst for education. Likewise, you could not stand behind the pulpit of a church unless you knew what you were going to teach. You had to find time to plan your sermon and study to show yourself approved by God, as Paul instructed: "Be diligent to present yourself approved to God, a worker who does not need to be ashamed, rightly dividing the word of truth" (2 Tim. 2.15).

Men like Apostle Paul had to spend many years under the feet of an esteemed professor of law called Gamaliel. The early Christians devoted themselves daily to public reading of the scriptures. The Berean Church examined the scriptures daily to see if what Paul was teaching was true (Acts 17.11). You had to pass the test. No wonder why the first century church was people that stood the test of time. No temptation or persecution could shake them because they were grounded in the faith. They believed and guarded their faith jealously from adulteration and corruption. I want you to see that success everywhere is based on certain principles and precepts.

The 1960s saw the walls of colonialism and imperialism, the fathers of oppression crumbling down. The fortress of apartheid in South Africa crumbled under the relentless desire of the population to experience freedom and live in an egalitarian society, where all people were deemed equal, and every form of life was cherished as dear and sacred. The relentless pursuit for freedom and equality of all humanity has increased and intensified generation after generation.

The cycle of oppression and stagnation is being broken, and the portals and frontiers of knowledge are advancing at an amazing rate. But how can you break the cycle of defeat unless you have the knowledge of how to do so? In this book, I offer you insight and understanding into how Satan has caged humanity in the vicious cycle of defeat, leaving men and women of all ages buttered and oppressed by the demands of human life.

Many people today are in the prison of depression and mental breakdown because so much pressure has been put on them. To truly address this, we must clearly study and search intently to understand why Satan seems to have so much power over humanity. God never intended for Satan to rule and reign, because God said, "Let Us make man in Our image, according to Our likeness; let them have dominion" (Gen. 1.26). Christ later came and declared "Behold, I give you the authority to trample on serpents and scorpions, and over all the power of the enemy" (Luke 10.19). It was power to break the cycle of defeat in every area of their life.

However, power is based on knowledge. Power without knowledge is no power at all. Humanity, out of ignorance, went out for power and not knowledge. Soon, their power, once challenged could not stand because it was zeal without knowledge. Knowledge is key. Solomon said, "Through wisdom a house is built, and by understanding it is established; by knowledge the rooms are filled with all precious and pleasant riches" (Prov. 24.3-4). Yet, in our generation, the quest for knowledge has waned. We have been offered the microwave and iPhone symbol of knowledge, but it is not knowledge itself.

Teach a man to fish, and you will have saved a generation; give him a fish, and you will have created a kingdom of beggars for posterity. In this book, I challenge you that you cannot destroy the cycle of defeat unless you first acquired knowledge about the cycle of defeat. What caused it? For how long has it been like this? How does it operate? What strategies can we use to fight it?

This book challenges you to develop a passion for real —an understanding of how Satan uses the cycle of defeat to assault human progress and advancements and caged nations, must be pursued with all your heart and mind. Creativity and progress are key pointers, yet I ask you a question: how many people today are spending time reading and studying? Social media gossip has captured our generation like a drug. We are all somehow addicted to it and a lot of time and resources are lost pursuing social media. Social media is like a steroid, we are captured, and we need to free ourselves like a gazelle. This is the challenge our generation must overcome to turn around the course of humanity.

Do you really have time to invest for your success? Success is not a matter of random chance but a crafted and deliberate pursuit of all that matters in life. It is a relentless pursuit of it, that one will only stop when they seize their goal.

As you read this book, understand that success, even the success of breaking the cycle of defeat, is based on certain principles and values that must inform and direct an individual's fight against the demonic and satanic cage. Among these principles, the management of one's mind ranks high in the priority of preparation and management.

William James (1842-1910) once made a life-changing statement that has challenged me over and over again. He said, "The greatest discovery of my generation is that a human being can alter his life by altering his attitude of mind." This profound truth reveals that you are where you are today because of your mindset. Your mind can either be a prison or a warrant of freedom, for as the Bible states, "For as he thinks in his heart, so is he" (Prov. 23.7). What you do with your mind determines what you will become.

This theme of the mind is one we will explore further in this book. Indeed, Henry David Thoreau (1817–1862) encapsulated this idea when he said, "If one advances confidently in the direction of his own dreams and endeavours to live the life which he has imagined, he will meet with a success unexpected in common hours." I will tell you again before we go far, that you ought to take care of your mind. Perhaps the greatest thing you ought to grasp as we read this book, is that it's all in the mind—your mind can either be a reservoir of fear or one of courage, it depends on what you decide by your own mind, to nurture and see to fruition.

The mind is like a forest; whatever you allow to grow will eventually fill it. You do not need a rocket scientist to understand. It is a matter of recognizing that the knowledge you acquire empowers you to act effectively and productively.

Someone once said, "Knowledge is knowing where to get information when you need it and then acting on it." Knowledge, therefore, is not just a tool but a weapon— a weapon that the fighter must always move with. It's not a kind of weapon you can put down even for a moment. Instead, knowledge must be tied up and fastened to your life like a belt, for it is indeed the "belt of truth" (Eph. 6.14). Knowledge is key.

However, to those who have fought to acquire knowledge, there is another thing you need to add to your knowledge. The apostle Peter advises us, "To knowledge, add self-control" (2 Pet.1.6). By the apostolic and prophetic wisdom God has given me, I say to you: in your fight against the cycle of defeat, to your knowledge, add principles.

You need to live a principled life, and many Christians do not have principles that inform and guard their life. Maybe you were screaming in your mind, "What is a principle? Why do I need it? Why should it be trust upon me at the beginning of this book?" Calm down, it is important that you get this, this is absolutely of first importance and must be grasped by everyone who is serious about breaking the cycle of defeat.

According to the Oxford English Dictionary, a principle is defined as "a fundamental truth or proposition that serves as a foundation for its system of belief or behaviour for its chain of reasoning." A principle, therefore, is a rule you live by, a belief you stand for and uphold, or an idea that guides the direction of your life. It acts as your road map or blueprint. Life must never be lived aimlessly; it must have meaning and purpose. It is principles that give your life it's meaning, purpose and uniqueness, shaping your destiny.

We must know what to believe in and why we believe in those things. These beliefs or principles become the standard by which we hold our lives accountable. Your fight against the cycle of defeat must acquire meaning and purpose if you are going to be motivated to fight it.

Nelson Mandela is a powerful example of a life driven by principle. He believed so much in the value and sanctity of freedom and equality. He held these ideals so dear to his heart and made it his lifelong goal and dream to free South Africa from the shackles of apartheid and human degradation. Mandela was willing to pay the ultimate price to obtain it, even if it meant losing his life in the process. He crafted a vision statement, which became the banner of his struggle against apartheid. It kept him alive and motivated, even during the 18 years he spent behind bars at Robben Island.

No amount of intimidation, torture, or persecution could break Mandela's indomitable spirit. His principles guided his struggle and shaped his discipline and desire to remain focus on the goal, no matter how long it would take. On 20 April 1964, during his Rivonia Trial and facing imprisonment or death, Mandela declared:

> "I have cherished the ideal of a democratic and free society. It is an ideal which I hope to live for and to achieve. But if needs be, it is an ideal for which I am prepared to die."

This is how sacrosanct Nelson Mandela held the ideal of democracy and a free Society after years of black subjugation and oppression. His life was bound to this principle. He could not move an inch unless his principles moved with him. He could not accept any compromise unless the compromise meant the fulfilment of his dream.

As Christians, we must be willing to defend our principles with the same steadfastness, defending them no matter the cost. Jesus Christ Himself was a man of principle and integrity. He was unwilling to compromise or alter the truth, no matter the pain and humiliation He would face. He was unwilling to change no matter the name-calling, the slander and the campaign of calumny against his life.

The magnanimity of Christ's character and the indomitability of His spirit are seen when He was facing death on the cross. In the Garden of Gethsemane, He cried out and said, "Father, if it is Your will, take this cup away from Me; nevertheless, not My will, but Yours, be done" (Luke 22.42). Christ's devotion to truth was unwavering. He was truth itself and could not deny Himself.

Groucho Marx, said, "Those are my principles, and if you don't like them, well, I have others." He was not saying that I would change my principles but highlighting that there are other people who are willing to accept them as they are. Similarly, President Jimmy Carter once said, "We must adjust to changing times and still hold to unchanging principles." This profound insight teaches that while methods may evolve, core principles must remain steadfast.

In order for you to fight against the cycle of defeat, it must be known from the onset that you need to choose your principles wisely. There is no better choice in life but to have principles bound by the word of God and led by the spirit of God. This is what many Christians are failing to do. If you fail to stand for something, you risk falling for anything. I have irked the anger of many people when I have refused to bend my principles.

I have read somewhere, that Napoleon Bonaparte remarked, "Great ambition is the passion of a great character. Those endowed with it may perform very good or very bad acts. All depends on the principles which direct them." This highlights the dual power of principles: they can either make us good people or bad people. Therefore, the formulation of life principles ought to be done with the greatest of care, conviction and clarity. They will carry your entire life either into eternity or eternal damnation.

Thomas S Monson gave this advice, "The principles of living greatly include the capacity to face trouble with courage, disappointment with cheerfulness, and trial with humility." We must understand without a shadow of a doubt, that God hates bondage and oppression. He is a God so powerful yet exercises his power so humbly. He is the mightiest, yet the most compassionate and forgiving. If God wants man to be free, it therefore means he hates the cycle of defeat because it does not represent his vision for humanity and mankind. If we, therefore, carefully pay attention to Him and His word, he will instruct us in such a way, through Knowledge and wisdom that Satan would never be able to cage us again and we would never spend another minute under the cycle of defeat.

Principles, however, are only as powerful as their application. Their power is seen when we put them into practice. It is in practice that we see the power of principle. Jesus emphasized this to His disciples, cautioning them to be doers of the Word and not hearers only. In Matthew 7.24-26, He says:

> "Therefore, whoever hears these sayings of Mine, and does them, I will liken him to a wise man who built his house on the rock: and the rain descended, the floods came, and the winds blew and beat on that house; and it did not fall, for it was founded on the rock. But everyone who hears these sayings of Mine, and does not do them, will be like a foolish man who built his house on the sand: and the rain descended, the floods came, and the winds blew and beat on that house; and it fell. And great was its fall."

A principle practiced is like a seed planted. If you water it, one day, it will spring to life. From the onset, make up your mind that what you will learn in this book, you will put into practice. It is not enough to know and to hold principles, it is necessary to put into effect your principles. Miracles are a product of action. What you do with what you know matters.

Oliver Wendell Holmes (1809-1894) said, "The great thing in this world is not so much where we are, but in what direction we are moving." It is not where we are that will determine where we will end up, but it is what we are doing that will be the determining factor of the outcome of our fight against the cycle of defeat. Every fight requires conviction, knowledge, enthusiasm, determination and faith; to be won.

You are holding and reading a rare book. It is in your hands, what you do with the knowledge you acquire, will tell us if you wasted your time or if it was worthwhile. As you read, you are stepping out into different realms of life and possibilities. Act upon what you are going to hear. Make up your mind and say to yourself, "It's time for action." Action brings revelation and revolution. Read on and your life will not be the same again.

2

Unmasking the Deceitfulness of Failure

I want to begin this booklet with a very serious approach. Paul warned Titus, "In everything set them an example by doing what is good. In your teaching show integrity, seriousness 8 and soundness of speech that cannot be condemned, so that those who oppose you may be ashamed because they have nothing bad to say about us." (Titus 2.7-8, NIV). Success in life belongs to those who are principled, self-disciplined and focused on their goals. These are people who are unwilling to be distracted or sidetracked by the enemy. They know what matters in life and why these things matter. They are also unwilling to engage in and fight the wrong battles.

The majority of believers end up defeated because they waste their energy and time fighting the wrong battles and the wrong enemy. They lack wisdom and are easily trapped by the devices of the enemy. You need to look at your life and consider how much time you have spent discussing problems and people, the energy and time wasted in arguing, striving, being angry, agitated, and frustrated. If you had chosen to focus on something positive, something inspiring, you could have shifted the trajectory of your destiny. In this booklet, I challenge you to rethink your past and relaunch your destiny from the beginning.

Understand that the following groups of people must bid farewell to success:

1. People who are obsessed with themselves and not with others (Phil. 2.4).
2. People who cannot handle criticism.
3. People who boast to show achievement and carry a spirit of spite.
4. People who cannot treat others properly.
5. People who are not honest with themselves and others.
6. People who carry envy and jealousy.
7. People with low self-esteem.
8. People who lack faith and trust.

Do not be one of them if you want to give your destiny a chance to succeed.

One Thing to Avoid

There is one thing everyone would like to avoid in their lifetime; it is the cycle of defeat. No one wants to encounter defeat in their life. Defeat is the most painful and shameful experience any human being would like to avoid at all costs. Yet, defeat confronts us every day—defeat in our personal lives, our health, business, careers, marriages, and even in our families. How can you avoid it? How can you defeat, defeat? Is it possible? Many people have committed suicide, some have been committed to mental institutions, and others are on some kind of antidepressants because they could not handle an experience of defeat.

In this booklet, I will share a secret with you on how you can break the cycle of defeat and rise to another level in your life. Psalms 34.19 says, "Many are the afflictions of the righteous, but the Lord delivers him out of them all." God wants to break the cycle of defeat in your life. Jeremiah 33.3 says, "Call to Me, and I will answer you, and show you great and mighty things, which you do not know." God wants to show you the secret of defeating and breaking the cycle of defeat so that you can live a victorious life as a Christian.

As the year draws to an end, this is a strategic time to rethink, reset, and position your life for victory. It is time to reflect and see how you can reposition yourself and avoid yesterday's cycle of defeat.

Step 1: Be mature and release your destiny and let the church grow.

It is important to recognize that no one can defeat the cycle of defeat unless they become mature. 2 Peter 3.18 says, "But grow in the grace and knowledge of our Lord and Saviour Jesus Christ. To Him be the glory both now and forever." Peter encourages us to grow and become mature. Maturity means being transformed into a greater state of being—becoming responsible, sensitive, sensible, helpful, fruitful, and productive. Mature Christians are full of the grace and knowledge of our Lord Jesus Christ. They have come to be like Christ in every way of their life.

Why should we be mature?

God will not release certain blessings or promote us unless we have matured to handle the blessing. Galatians 4.1-3 explains that an heir, as long as they are a child, is no different from a slave, even though they are the owner of everything. Because they are not mature, God will not release the blessing meant for them. By becoming mature, we qualify for the blessing of God.

What standard or level of maturity is God looking for?

Ephesians 4.13-16 states that we must reach unity in the faith and attain the whole measure of the fullness of Christ. We must grow and be mature, so we are no longer like children—unstable and unreliable. We must grow until each one of us does our part in the work of the Kingdom of God.

How do we grow?

1 Peter 2.2 says, "As newborn babes, desire the pure milk of the word, that you may grow thereby." You need to spend time reading your Bible and attending church services to grow and be mature. Stop being elementary. You need to leave behind the basic tenets of Christianity and go on to maturity (Heb. 6.1-4).

As a mature believer, learn to handle difficult situations and do not avoid them. Hebrews 5.14 says, "But solid food belongs to those who are of full age, that is, those who by reason of use have their senses exercised to discern both good and evil."

What is our strategy to break the cycle of defeat? Reset, regroup and recover

We cannot defeat the cycle of defeat unless we reset our minds. Romans 12.2 says, "And do not be conformed to this world, but be transformed by the renewing of your mind." Your mindset is important as a weapon to defeat the cycle of defeat. You need to think right. You become what you think about yourself and your situation. Be convinced that you can make it. When we are facing defeat, many things in our lives tend to be scattered.

Therefore, regroup—gather yourself back together and relaunch yourself. Once you have regrouped, fight to recover what you have lost to the enemy. By taking this approach, we will change our perspective, adjust ourselves, and focus on what brings us victory. If you want to know more about this, please ask for the following books:

1. The Secret of Achieving Dominion
2. Breaking the Cycle of Defeat
3. How to Make Your Dream Come True

Congratulations! You are on your path to success. See your victory and believe in it.

The last thing you need to learn is to pray. You cannot succeed in life unless you have learned to pray—consistently and strategically. Prayer is such a powerful weapon in the hands of a believer that, when handled properly, it has tremendous power to change everything in the believer's life. This year will be the best year of your life. It's your comeback experience. Be sure to be righteous and obey the Word of God. Your life will never be the same again. Your journey starts now—step out in faith and take hold of your victory through Jesus Christ. There is enough anointing and power to carry you through. I see you stepping out in total victory. You are going to amaze many people. You are going to shock and surprise yourself. You will release what you never thought you had. You are the miracle on the horizon. You are the testimony God has been eager to release. Now, here you are. Do not be afraid. Believe and act on your faith.

Sum it up

1. Think rationally and not emotionally. Emotional thinking is destructive (Rom. 8. 5-6)
2. Plan and follow your plan always (Luke. 14.28)
3. Manage your time wisely starting by tightly managing your daily routine. Time is valuable (Eph. 5.16)
4. Believe in yourself and in what God has put in you. (Phil. 4.13)
5. Just be yourself
6. Trust God an do not lean on your understanding (Prov. 3.5-6)

3

Your Mindset as Key

Breaking the cycle of defeat is an essential battle every Christian must fight. The struggle to rise above and beyond the limits of defeat is central to victorious Christian living. It is crucial for every Christian to understand what was on God's mind when He created humanity. What kind of creature did God create? Why did He create humanity in this way? These are key questions that must be answered, but they must be addressed within the context of the entire creation story.

We are told in Genesis 1.31, "Then God saw everything that He had made, and indeed it was very good. So the evening and the morning were the sixth day." God is a master planner and a master creator. He creates masterpieces for Himself and for His own glory. God's creation is glorious because it was meant to bring Him glory. We can be certain that God did not create anything substandard or mediocre. How could this magnificent God create something that would not reflect the excellence of His character and nature?

When God created humanity, He left no room for doubt or speculation about what He intended humans to be. It is stated clearly in Genesis 1.26-28: "Then God said, 'Let Us make man in Our image, according to Our likeness; let them have dominion over the fish of the sea, over the birds of the air, and over the cattle, over all the earth and over every creeping thing that creeps on the earth.' So God created man in His own image; in the image of God He created him; male and female He created them. Then God blessed them, and God said to them, 'Be fruitful and multiply; fill the earth and subdue it; have dominion over the fish of the sea, over the birds of the air, and over every living thing that moves on the earth.'"

It is important to pause here and reflect prayerfully on how the Bible describes the creation of humanity. What did God want us to know about the man or woman He created? Why was it important for God to reveal this information about the creation of human beings? I will return shortly to share my revelation on this matter, but we must first take a close look at Genesis 1.26-28. This passage is a body of instructive information that cannot be taken lightly.

For centuries, the creation story has been repeated and recited without serious thought given to its significance. What are its theological footprints for the history and state of the human race? How can we use this story to interpret and offer a detailed analysis of God's plan and blueprint, and how humanity ought to handle it in order to benefit from the Kingdom God created for us? This story also reveals the true spiritual identity of human beings and how the lack of understanding of this has led to the cycle of defeat that is suffocating humanity across the globe. Unless humanity understands God's original intent and design, we will continue to experience defeat, setbacks, and disappointment throughout our time on Earth.

Peter reminds us, "as His divine power has given to us all things that pertain to life and godliness, through the knowledge of Him who called us by glory and virtue, by which have been given to us exceedingly great and precious promises, that through these you may be partakers of the divine nature, having escaped the corruption that is in the world through lust" (2 Pet. 1.3-4). Here, we find astonishing insight into God's mindset toward humanity.

Genesis 1.26-28 must be thoroughly examined and laid bare to bring understanding to humanity of God's design and plan.

1. "Let Us make man in Our image, according to Our likeness." What is "image"? What is "likeness"? What, then, is the image and likeness that God is referring to?
2. "Let them have dominion"—that is, let humanity rule.

3. God blessed humanity and said, "Be fruitful and multiply; fill the earth and subdue it."

Having identified three critical aspects of the creation story—a preview of God's idea of humanity—we must now consider what it means for humanity to know God's intention. God created humanity in His image and likeness. Here, we have two key terms: "image" and "likeness." It is imperative to define what "image" means and what God's image signifies.

The term "image" can be understood both generally and specifically, particularly as it relates to the image of God. According to the Oxford Language Dictionary, "image" is defined as "a representation of the external form of a person or thing in art." It can also mean "the general impression that a person, organization, or product presents to the public." Many parents are delighted to have a baby, but they are even more joyful when the baby resembles them—and not the man next door. A man desires his child, conceived from his own loins, to be like him. There is great joy for a father when he is told, "Your son or daughter is just like you."

God created humanity in His image and likeness because humans were specially marked out and set apart for God's glory. He made them male and female in His image and likeness. Humanity had to be special for God to choose them to be made or created in His image. But what is God's image? The image of God, or *Imago Dei*, is a theological term uniquely applied to humans, denoting the symbolic relationship between God and humanity. The term has its roots in Genesis 1.27, where "God created man in His own image." This scriptural passage does not imply that God is in human form but rather that humans reflect the image of God in their moral, spiritual, and intellectual nature.

Thus, humans mirror God's divinity through their ability to actualize the unique qualities with which they have been endowed, setting them apart from all other creatures. The term Imago Dei refers fundamentally to two things: God's own self-actualization through humankind and God's care for humankind. To say that humans are in the image of God is to acknowledge the special qualities of human nature that allow God to manifest in them. Simply put, it is to recognize that humanity holds a special position in God's heart: "He is the apple of His eye" (Ps. 17.8). We are further reminded, "What is man that You are mindful of him?" (Ps. 8.4). Humanity is "fearfully and wonderfully made" (Ps. 139.14).

Man was God's final creation. God did His best and created humanity to be "a chosen generation, a royal priesthood, a holy nation, His own special people, that you may proclaim the praises of Him who called you out of darkness into His marvellous light" (1 Pet. 2.9). That was no small feat. God declared that you will be "a kingdom of priests" (Exod. 19.6). In battles, God assures the person He created, "Yet in all these things we are more than conquerors through Him who loved us" (Rom. 8.37). Since God is for you, nobody can be against you. Humanity can rest assured of God's perfect will for them. "You are the head and not the tail" (Deut. 28.13).

What blessed assurance from the Lord! Paul declares that "nothing in all creation shall be able to separate us from the love of God which is in Christ Jesus our Lord" (Rom. 8.39). In Christ, humanity was given the ability and authority, empowered by God, to stand victoriously no matter what comes their way. Therefore, be anxious for nothing. God has already provided the necessary provisions and protection you need: "As His divine power has given to us all things that pertain to life and godliness, through the knowledge of Him who called us by glory and virtue" (2 Pet. 1.3).

God has not left humanity's security and the guarantee of freedom to chance or to the whims of man. Rather, He declared that whom He foreknew, He also predestined to be conformed to the image of Christ. Are you listening? Do you understand what God has already done for you? God is not trying to secure your destiny—He has already secured it.

God intended for humanity to have dominion, that is, the power to rule, subdue what comes their way, and be in charge and control. Yet, in today's world, people are overwhelmed by the pressures of life. There is a critical mental breakdown, and psychological pressures that has driven God's victorious creation into mental institutions and to the over-reliance on antidepressants. Why have people accepted this lower status? Why has humanity downgraded itself and taken on a lesser form? This is not an act of humility but of desperation and despondency.

Yet, God said in Genesis 1.28, "Then God blessed them, and God said to them, 'Be fruitful and multiply; fill the earth and subdue it.'" But look at people on buses going to work—they're not happy, overshadowed by gloom and sadness. People wear long faces. What has happened to humanity? Why do we seem cursed when we are blessed? Where do we begin to adjust? Surely, there must be a starting point, as God had a starting point. How do we get back on track? How do we place our lives back on the pedestal of God's blueprint?

God calls out, saying, "For I know the thoughts that I think toward you, says the Lord, thoughts of peace and not of evil, to give you a future and a hope" (Jer. 29.11). How do we reconnect with this plan? God continues, "Call to Me, and I will answer you, and show you great and mighty things, which you do not know" (Jer. 33.3). Clearly, people do not know. But how do we start? How did Satan start? How did God start?

God began with His mind: "Then God said, 'Let Us make man in Our image, according to Our likeness; let them have dominion...'" (Gen. 1.26). Satan, too, began in his heart and mind, saying, "I will be like the Most High" (Isa. 14.14). Thoughts are like seeds—whatever you plant will one day germinate and reveal itself. Therefore, we must start with our mind. There is a significant term we must now explore: mindset. This term comprises two keywords: "mind" and "set."

Our mind is the citadel of our thoughts, and our thoughts are the seeds that shape our lives. To "set" means to put something in order, to align it correctly, to frame it so that it can be used properly and effectively. What are you thinking right now? Your thoughts will either make or break you. We need to watch our thoughts carefully. Is your mindset properly established? Do you have the right frame of mind?

Your mind is like a roof; if the roof of a house is leaking, the entire house is in danger of being destroyed. A leaking roof can ruin everything inside a house or building. Similarly, a leaking mind has the power to destroy virtually everything in one's life. Even great men and women have sometimes been destroyed by the destructive patterns of their thinking habits. Paul advises us to "be transformed by the renewing of your mind" (Rom. 12.2). To experience renewal in your life, your mind must be renewed—there are no shortcuts here. As Proverbs 23.7 says, "For as he thinks in his heart, so is he." What you spend your time thinking about, that is what you will become.

Henry Ford once said, "If you think you can do a thing or think you can't do a thing, you're right." Paul warns in Romans 8.6, "For to be carnally minded is death, but to be spiritually minded is life and peace." To break the cycle of defeat, start by addressing your thinking pattern. What drives your thoughts? What motivates or inspires your thoughts?

Someone once said, "You can take a boy out of the farm, but you cannot take the farm out of the boy's mind." Sometimes, what is deeply embedded in our lives can destroy every opportunity God gives and subject us to relentless failure and defeat. If we allow unscriptural habits of thinking, we will kill everything God has given us. Start where it matters most—your mind.

No one can be bitter and contentious unless they have allowed their mind to be poisoned by the chalice of bitterness, anger, and resentment. It does not matter what happens; even angels can come, but a poisoned mind will see angels as if they are demons. Your greatest benefactors may appear to be your enemies. A poisoned mind is a danger to its owner and a poison to its neighbours.

The many miracles we have seen and read about were once conceived in the mind of a person. The great discoveries and revolutions that have radically affected humanity started in the mind of someone who refused to give up their thoughts despite opposition and persecution. The freedom for Black people in America was nurtured in the minds of great civil rights leaders like Martin Luther King Jr. The end of apartheid was conceived and nurtured in prisons in the minds of great South African leaders like Nelson Mandela, Oliver Tambo, Robert Sobukwe, Steve Biko, and Chris Hani. These men, along with their female counterparts, risked their lives for freedom—but it was a freedom first conceived in their minds. It was nurtured in their minds and put into action by their minds.

Great biblical characters like Joseph defied opposition to serve their nation. Daniel resolved in his mind and heart that he would not defile himself (Dan. 1.8). Once his mind was made up, no amount of threats, persecution, or torture could deter him. A made-up mind is a lethal weapon against the forces of darkness and any demonic fortress. It is a key that unlocks Satan's gates and frees humanity from the bondage of Satan. Watch how you think.

To influence your thoughts wisely, read the Word of God. The Word of God has the capacity and capability to renew your mind. It can detox your mind, purge it, and reset you for victory. There is no wall of Jericho that a renewed mind cannot penetrate. Your mindset matters more than anything else. It is not the size of your battle that matters; it is the size of your mind.

The den of lions could not intimidate Daniel, whose mind was made up. A fiery furnace became inconsequential for Shadrach, Meshach, and Abednego because their minds were made up (Dan. 3.16-18). There are no shortcuts and no magic wands—gird the loins of your mind. Your mindset is the combustion chamber where your life is forged. Take care of your mind, and the cycle of defeat will bow on the altar of a determined mind.

You have the mind of Christ (1 Cor. 2.16). You can do all things through Christ who strengthens you (Phil. 4.13). Like Esther, with a mind made up, do not be afraid to face challenges. Esther said, "I will go to the king, which is against the law; and if I perish, I perish!" (Esth. 4.16). That is the resolve of a determined mind.

Your mind is a fortress. It is a laser beam that can cut through any hindrance. As you make up your mind, the cycle of defeat will crumble before you. The demons of defeat, setbacks, and disappointment will flee from your presence, allowing you to enjoy the life God intended for you. Through prayer, your mind can be renewed. Through prayer, your feeble mind can rise up to any challenge. This is the secret to breaking and overcoming the cycle of defeat. Do not wait for tomorrow or for a convenient time. Make up your mind now and step out in faith.

In life, you can either become bitter or better. Your destiny is waiting for you to make up your mind. God is waiting for you to decide; when you do, He will back you up 100%. Stop entertaining thoughts of fear and worry. Stop anxious thoughts—they are a poison. Step out in faith. I will end this part with this Scripture: "Therefore do not cast away your confidence, which has great reward. For you have need of endurance, so that after you have done the will of God, you may receive the promise" (Heb. 10.35-36).

We discuss at length how crucial our mindset is. It determines whether we succeed or fail in life. As we continue examining this aspect, we must ask, "How can I defeat the cycle of defeat? How can I overcome the cycle of defeat?" These questions highlight two dynamic aspects of human life. First, they acknowledge that humanity faces a challenge: the cycle of defeat. In other words, being trapped in a cycle of defeat is a reality we witness daily. We see Christians repeatedly experiencing this cycle. Some are defeated in their marriages, with broken relationships and rising divorce rates. It's an undeniable part of life.

Another Christian may be locked in a cycle of poor health, leaving us to wonder what happened or what is happening. Others may be caught in a cycle of debt that endlessly repeats itself. Naturally, we ask: "How can I overcome this? How can I escape this shame? What can I do to change this?" Wouldn't you want an answer? I'm sure, like everyone else, you would sigh with relief if you found one. And I assure you, there is an answer. I am here to show you the secret of defeating this cycle. But hold on for a moment. Don't be anxious. I want to be systematic, logical, and comprehensive in sharing this secret. It's a secret that will change your life and give you leverage; where others have failed you will succeed, where someone else found disappointment, you will find appointment.

Remember this: "Through wisdom a house is built, and by understanding it is established; by knowledge the rooms are filled with all precious and pleasant riches" (Prov. 24.3-4). These three key elements—wisdom, understanding, and knowledge—unlock the secret. Do you desire these in your daily life? My concern is to share with you this secret, and I certainly will. But first, let's revisit the second aspect of overcoming the cycle of defeat. This aspect assumes that the cycle should not be a part of a Christian's life.

It is not God's will for you to be trapped in defeat. Consider the following Scriptures to understand God's intentions for humanity. What did God envision for the person He created in Genesis 1? He gave a clear identity and purpose for how that life would be reflected. Genesis 1.26-28 states, "Then God said, 'Let Us make man in Our image, according to Our likeness; let them have dominion over the fish of the sea, over the birds of the air, and over the cattle, over all the earth and over every creeping thing that creeps on the earth.' So God created man in His own image; in the image of God He created him; male and female He created them. Then God blessed them, and God said to them, 'Be fruitful and multiply; fill the earth and subdue it;

have dominion over the fish of the sea, over the birds of the air, and over every living thing that moves on the earth.'"

Reflect on how this promise connects with what God says in Jeremiah 29.11: "'For I know the thoughts that I think toward you,' says the Lord, 'thoughts of peace and not of evil, to give you a future and a hope.'" Moreover, 2 Peter 1.3-4 declares, "As His divine power has given to us all things that pertain to life and godliness, through the knowledge of Him who called us by glory and virtue, by which have been given to us exceedingly great and precious promises, that through these you may be partakers of the divine nature, having escaped the corruption that is in the world through lust." Also, 3 John 1.2 reminds us, "Beloved, I pray that you may prosper in all things and be in health, just as your soul prospers."

God has given us great and precious promises, so we may enter into divine communion and achieve the unexpected and the impossible. Satan, however, seeks to hide the reality of God's blueprint and vision for our lives. He wants us to see lack, not abundance; suffering, not the glory behind it; defeat, not the breakthrough beyond it. It is Satan's nature to deceive and blind us to the reality of God's promises, while God's will is to reveal the hidden things that make us knowledgeable and effective.

Consider what God said of Abraham in Genesis 18.17-19, where He reveals His plans because of Abraham's righteousness:

> "And the Lord said, 'Shall I hide from Abraham what I am doing, since Abraham shall surely become a great and mighty nation, and all the nations of the earth shall be blessed in him? For I have known him, in order that he may command his children and his household after him, that they keep the way of the Lord, to do righteousness and justice, that the Lord may bring to Abraham what He has spoken to him." (Gen.18.17-19)

Galatians 3.17 further explains that the covenant God made with Abraham remains valid: "And this I say, that the law, which was four hundred and thirty years later, cannot annul the covenant that was confirmed before by God in Christ, that it should make the promise of no effect." And as Amos 3.7 tells us: "Surely the Lord God does nothing, unless He reveals His secret to His servants the prophets."

God promises that the yoke shall be broken because of the anointing (Isa. 10.27). You are anointed by God, so any yoke Satan tries to place upon you or your life will be broken. I do not understand why you do not yet see that God has made you more than a conqueror and given you the power to stand in total victory. You are a child of God, and with His anointing, you are equipped to break the cycle of defeat and walk in triumph.

This is God's plan, and it is made clear in His Word. What is stopping you from attaining the greatness He has desired and designed for you? God has provided all the resources you need to overcome. So, why not step out in faith? Why is your life confined to the boat of familiarity and your comfort zone? God may shake your comfort zone to force you out of a debilitating environment— when you seem free, but are actually bound. What's the problem? Why are you going in circles all the time?

Let me tell you: the problem is simple, yet complicated. It's the mindset—period. Your mind is set in such a way that it halts reason and rationality. I'll come back to this point later. But for now, let's go back to the beginning. Whenever you seem to be failing repeatedly, there's power in returning to the start. The beginning of things often reveals the end, if we think critically and creatively. Christians are not exempt from critical thinking. Isaiah 1.18-19 says, "'Come now, and let us reason together,' says the Lord." God invites us into a dialogue—a dialogue immersed in the waters of reason.

The devil has placed you in a valley, but that is not your place, nor your portion. Pause and reflect: how can you come out? Reason creates a ladder by which you can climb out of the valley of the shadow of death, despair, and hopelessness.

The third aspect of this matrix is that God wants you to destroy the cycle of defeat in your life. Through His Word, God has promised how you can accomplish this. That's how much He cares about you and the outcome of your trials and struggles. At best, God wants to turn your tests into testimonies, your trials into triumphs, and your struggles into breakthroughs. God is doing a new thing in your life—He wants to end the old picture of the cycle of defeat. But the question remains: how can you do this? Is it even possible? What does it take to achieve it?

God has already demonstrated that with Him, all things are possible—if you exercise faith. To believe God is to see beyond human experience and understanding. It is to enter the realm of faith and revolution, which one can only reach through true and unshaken faith. This spiritual realm is one you must enter to access heavenly deposits and guarantees. It's a realm of supernatural activity, surpassing the natural world of limitations and despair.

So, how does one activate this? How does one open the spiritual doors of this realm? God has blessed me with supernatural spiritual knowledge and sensitivity, and I say, "I know, and I know that I know." Your mindset is a springboard for many supernatural activities and openings. The state of your mind is critical in knowing God's will.

What state of mind must you have to contact God, and how do you connect to the divine? This question has perplexed intellectuals, scientists, and theologians for centuries. In a few moments, I will bring clarity to this question, enhancing your chances to step forward into the supernatural realm. Resetting your mind is unavoidable; it is a necessary step to enter into communion with God and access heavenly deposits. This life is much more than what meets the eye—it begins with how you set your mind, what I call "mind setting."

Colossians 3.2 says, "Set your mind on things above, not on things on the earth." You must take a step of faith, renew your mind, and deliberately and intentionally create a set focus. Your mind must transcend the pleasures of the natural or fleshly realm and move toward a heavenly dimension, seeing what Christ desires and how He has positioned Himself vis a vis heaven. Our daily focus often shifts toward our natural needs, but what is spiritually set for us through the death and resurrection of Jesus Christ is of far greater importance.

Prayer and meditation usher us into that realm, but it must be intense, fervent, and reverent prayer before God. It is a prayer in which one ceases to see oneself but sees God more and more—a state in which one obtains a serene mind, whose sole preoccupation is communion with God. One cannot achieve this while distracted or carnally minded. Romans 8.6 says, "For to be carnally minded is death, but to be spiritually minded is life and peace."

God is bringing a spiritual revolution to our generation by regenerating our mindsets. Anxious and worrisome thoughts are like mist in a man's eyes, preventing clarity and spiritual visibility.

God challenges us to stop being double-minded. Double-mindedness is a spiritual block, hindering and disturbing the work of the Spirit.

Spiritual thinking or spirit-led thinking, is not common in our generation, but it is essential. There is a state of being where a person reflects Christ alone, completely lost in Him. It is a spiritual position that one attains by cleansing oneself of human prejudice and suspicion. When the mind is corrupted by the world and the works of the flesh, trust and belief in oneself—or even in others—become unattainable. This higher state of being transcends envy, jealousy, self-ambition, anger, and satanic manipulations. The Holy Spirit is our schoolmaster, professor, and mighty counsellor, showing us how to transform our minds to attain the mind of Christ and release us from the clutches of death and leads us into the fullness of life.

The quality of our thinking inevitably affects the quality and state of our decision-making. It is impossible to have a poor thinking pattern and somehow attain a high level of effective decision-making.

Thus, renewing our minds in line with God's will is critical to achieving the supernatural life He has intended for us.

David Schwartz, in *The Magic of Thinking Big*, emphasizes the transformative power of thinking expansively. As Schwartz's vice president stated, "The difference is that Harry thought five times bigger." Success, as Schwartz suggests, is not about the size of one's brain, but rather the magnitude of one's thinking. This principle leads us to question: if big thinking can accomplish so much, why don't more people adopt it? Let me answer this question and show you a secret. Remember, the reason why I am writing is to show a hidden mystery of what makes a Christian life a masterpiece for God's glory.

While David Schwartz attributes much of success to what he calls "the magic of thinking big," I must clarify that from a Christian perspective, this so-called "magic" is not what drives the faithful toward great achievements. As a staunch conservative and classical Christian, I do not agree with or align with the notion of magic. God, not magic, shapes our destiny, and His methods are vastly different from what Schwartz portrays. The divine blueprint does not rely on mystical or human concepts of "magic." Instead, God reveals to us the secrets of how we can think big, guided by faith and His Word. Unlike magic, which is associated with Satan, God's guidance is rooted in His promises and truths.

God's design for His children involves doing the impossible using the gift of their mind. Consider how, with a made-up mind, David survived persecution and harassment and eventually became king, and how Joseph overcame the plot of Potiphar's wife to rise to the position of Prime Minister in Egypt. In both cases, it was not magic, but God's favor, wisdom, and the ability to think beyond their immediate circumstances that led to their success.

People are often obsessed with size and quantity, but God cares more about stewardship and effectiveness. He is the God of wonders, miracles, and the impossible. How you think matters far more than the size of your brain or the extent of your education. In today's generation, we see people who act more on emotion and the flesh, which only underscores the need for a shift in mindset. The time and attention you invest in a subject matter often determine the quality of the outcome.

God calls us to think more and think big. We must not be intimidated by what we see or hear in the natural. Acting out of faith in God creates a springboard for success. What might appear as a hurdle or roadblock can become a stepping stone to victory. Your perceived threats, when confronted with God-given wisdom and courage, can become anchors that lead you to success.

The Bible declares, "For you have the mind of Christ" (1 Cor. 2.16). This is the true secret behind thinking big in a way that glorifies God. It's not about human achievement or intellect but about aligning your mind with the thoughts and purposes of Christ. As you read this book and continue your journey, remember to think big—but not in the way the world might suggest. Think big through the lens of faith, knowing that with God, nothing is impossible.

The next chapter, which I will share with you, reveals how you can create a leverage using your mind. Are you ready? Because what comes next will blow your mind, opening up new horizons of faith and possibility.

4

Understanding the Essence of the Battle

In the last chapter, we talked about the mind and mindset, exploring what we are thinking, how we are thinking, and why we think the way we do. Your thinking pattern plays a crucial role in breaking the cycle of defeat. Learning to think clearly and efficiently is essential if you want to map out a strategy that leads to victory. This is what I call *strategic thinking*—a type of thinking in which you learn to devise a plan for how you will approach the battle and win it. You are not simply fighting; you are fighting with a mindset focused on victory. What plan have you put in place to fight and combat your enemy? How will you implement and execute this plan to ensure success? It is not enough to just engage in battle or to fight aimlessly. I am a strategic thinker, a disciplined and focused soldier who has learned to carefully assess the fight, the terrain in which the battle takes place, and the tools required to achieve victory.

Many people do not perceive life correctly. There is one essential and significant understanding we all need: our view of life shapes how we live it, manage it, and fulfil it. The Word of God offers us the correct view of life, and we must embrace it to fight and win, leading to a successful life. Proverbs 3.5-6 declares, "Trust in the Lord with all your heart, and lean not on your own understanding; in all your ways acknowledge Him, and He shall direct your paths." This passage is testament to the idea that we did not create ourselves—God did. If our personal thoughts are contrary to God's mindset, we will not be able to withstand life's challenges and storms. The only hope is to fashion your mind after the mind of God. This is possible by surrendering your mind to God.

Romans 12.2 emphasizes, "And do not be conformed to this world, but be transformed by the renewing of your mind, that you may prove what is that good and acceptable and perfect will of God." Why is it necessary to understand God's perfect will? Because I owe everything to God. He designed me, and I am His creation. He directs my daily steps to fulfil the purpose for which He created me. Psalm 23:3 states, "He leads me in the paths of righteousness for His name's sake." God, as my shepherd, must lead me because he knows the way, He knows why He created me and what He intends for me to accomplish. Therefore, my mind must align with His mind. My life will only function properly when my thoughts conform to His will.

This is not easy in your everyday life. It is difficult and challenging—it is the narrow path where one must surrender their own will and accept God's will. Thus, a constant battle exists, a continual pull in the opposite direction. Life, therefore, is a battle. The Word of God presents life as an ongoing battle. From the moment Satan fell from heaven, a war has been raging between the armies of God and the forces of Satan. Whether you can see it with your physical eyes or not, the battle is happening. Even if you prefer not to engage in it, the enemy is already attacking. If you do not fight, the enemy of your life will not stop fighting you.

1 Peter 5.8 warns, "Be sober, be vigilant; because your adversary the devil walks about like a roaring lion, seeking whom he may devour." Since the battle at Calvary, when Christ died, descended into the abyss of hell, fought with the devil and seized his sword, the enemy has been defeated and wounded. Yet, despite being wounded, he persists until the time of his final annihilation. Know the battle is for real. It's happening now.

In Psalms 18.39, we are told, "For You have armed me with strength for the battle; You have subdued under me those who rose up against me." It is clear that God has already equipped you with the strength for this battle and that those who rise against you, including the cycle of defeat, will be defeated. David cried out in Psalm 144.1, "Blessed be the Lord my Rock, who trains my hands for war, and my fingers for battle." This makes it evident that God does not leave you alone in the battle. God personally trains you to fight the battle because His ultimate desire is for you to emerge victorious. God would not invest time in training you if He did not care whether you win or lose. His plan is for you to win, and He does the necessary preparation to ensure that you are well-equipped for battle.

Do you understand that life is a battle and a constant one? This is an important question for you. It is a question you must grapple with and understand. Clarity to this question is a clarion call for every believer. Your mindset must be configured in certain way if you are going to act in a proper way. Know this as you read this book, that life is a BATTLE. It is a real battle and the battle is taking place now. You are in the battle and your adversary the devil has marked you because he wants you to lose the battle.

This should be your mindset. Now that you understand that life is a battle, Do you also understand what kind of a battle? Life is not just any battle—it is spiritual in nature. We can't simply go about fighting aimlessly, without any aim; we need to understand the kind of battle we're engaged in. Understanding the type of battle helps you to determine how you will fight the battle and with what strategy. Choose your battles wisely. Some battles are worth fighting, others are inconsequential, and some are mere distractions. Just as an experienced army general takes a lot of time to study the possibilities of battle, carefully analyzing data, weighing the advantages and disadvantages of engaging in combat, and then he makes crafted and calibrated decisions to make sure that the battalion will engage only in battles that give the army the maximum benefit; you too must choose which battles to fight—through the wisdom of God, not your own understanding.

Ephesians 6.12-18 explains: "For we do not wrestle against flesh and blood, but against principalities, against powers, against the rulers of the darkness of this age, against spiritual hosts of wickedness in the heavenly places. Therefore, take up the whole armor of God, that you may be able to withstand in the evil day, and having done all, to stand. Stand therefore, having girded your waist with truth, having put on the breastplate of righteousness, and having shod your feet with the preparation of the gospel of peace; above all, taking the shield of faith with which you will be able to quench all the fiery darts of the wicked one. And take the helmet of salvation, and the sword of the Spirit, which is the word of God." God clearly defines our battle as spiritual, not carnal. We are not fighting against flesh and blood but against spiritual forces—powers, principalities, spiritual wickedness in high places and rulers of darkness.

God has defined our battle, so it would be unwise for a Christian to defy God's matrix of understanding of the battle we must fight. Additionally, God exhorts us to take courage when we are fighting this battle. The right attitude to carry into battle is courage, as demonstrated by David in 1 Samuel 17.47: "Then all this assembly shall know that the Lord does not save with sword and spear; for the battle is the Lord's, and He will give you into our hands." The believer must Understand that he must engage in the battle against the cycle of defeat courageously. As believers, we must recognize that while we engage in the battle, the victory ultimately belongs to God. He fights for us, and our part is to trust in Him and acknowledge that He is in control.

Moses also reassures us in Deuteronomy 20.4: "For the Lord your God is He who goes with you, to fight for you against your enemies, to save you." No matter the nature, size, or timing of the battle, there Is one thing guaranteed—if you believe in God, He will fight for you and bring you victory.

Apart from defining the battle, the Lord has also chosen the weapons of our warfare. As 2 Corinthians 10.4 reminds us, "For the weapons of our warfare are not carnal but mighty in God for pulling down strongholds." These weapons are neither natural nor physical; they are spiritual. Many people lose their battles because they are using the wrong weapons for the specific battle they are facing. In Ephesians 6, we are instructed on the specific weapons we should use—the whole armor of God. This includes the belt of truth, the breastplate of righteousness, the shoes of the gospel of peace, the helmet of salvation, the shield of faith, and the sword of the Spirit. Each of these spiritual tools is essential for victory in the believer's life. In a short while, I will go into greater detail about the importance of these weapons and how they are vital in fighting against the cycle of defeat.

God has already chosen the tools you need and how you can use them to break the cycle of defeat in your life. Choosing the right tools and using them effectively can truly transform your spiritual life, making the difference between failure and success. God hasn't left us guessing about what tools to use—He has handpicked them and handed them over, saying, "Here are the tools you need for this type of battle." Now let's return to Ephesians 6.10-17:

> "Finally, my brethren, be strong in the Lord and in the power of His might. Put on the whole armor of God, that you may be able to stand against the wiles of the devil. For we do not wrestle against flesh and blood, but against principalities, against powers, against the rulers of the darkness of this age, against spiritual hosts of wickedness in the heavenly places. Therefore take up the whole armor of God, that you may be able to withstand in the evil day, and having done all, to stand. Stand therefore, having girded your waist with truth, having put on the breastplate of righteousness, and having shod your feet with the preparation of the gospel of peace; above all, taking the shield of faith with which you will be able to quench all the fiery darts of the wicked one. And take the helmet of salvation, and the sword of the Spirit, which is the word of God."

The passage warns Christians about the nature of the battle: it is spiritual. Therefore, the weapons cannot be physical; they must also be spiritual. This is worth repeating because of its importance. As Philippians 3.1 reminds us, "For me to write the same things to you is not tedious, but for you it is safe."

The Armor of God

The first weapon you must put on is the full armor of God. Notice it says *full armor*, not just any armor. The Oxford Dictionary defines armor as "the metal coverings formerly worn by soldiers to protect the body in battle." Similarly, in our spiritual battle against Satan, who wants to trap us in cycles of defeat, we need to take on the armor of God.

Psalms 91.1-2 assures us: "He who dwells in the secret place of the Most High shall abide under the shadow of the Almighty. I will say of the Lord, 'He is my refuge and my fortress; my God, in Him I will trust.'" We must be hidden in God, immersing ourselves completely in Him, so that we are protected from the enemy's attacks. Our entire body must be covered by the spiritual covering of God's Word to avoid being exposed to the enemy. In Christ, we have our ultimate defense.

The Belt of Truth

The second piece of spiritual armor is the belt of truth. The devil is described as the father of lies in John 8.44 "You are of your father the devil, and the desires of your father you want to do. He was a murderer from the beginning and does not stand in the truth, because there is no truth in him. When he speaks a lie, he speaks from his own resources, for he is a liar and the father of it." Those who belong to the Satanic Kingdom rely entirely on lies and manipulation to deceive and destroy God's chosen people. However, Jesus gives us a different promise. In John 8.32, He declares, "And you shall know the truth, and the truth shall make you free." Jesus Himself is the truth, and truth is found only in Him; it is His nature. He affirms this in John 14.6: "I am the way, the truth, and the life. No one comes to the Father except through Me." Without knowing and living in the truth of God's Word, it is impossible to defeat the cycle of defeat or to overcome the devil. When a believer lives in the truth and upholds the truth set forth in the Word of God, the cycle of defeat literally melts in the presence of the truth.

The Breastplate of Righteousness

The third weapon in the spiritual battle is the breastplate of righteousness. According to the Oxford Dictionary, righteousness is defined as "the state of being morally right or justifiable." Spiritually, righteousness means being in right standing with God—being acceptable to Him. Psalms 19.14 declares, "Let the words of my mouth and the meditation of my heart be acceptable in Your sight, O Lord, my strength and my Redeemer." If God accepts you, no one can stand against you. This assurance is reinforced in Romans 8.31, "If God is for us, who can be against us?" There is an absolute guarantee of victory if God is on our side. We cannot bribe or deceive God. He is persuaded by righteousness, which is His very nature. Proverbs 14.34 says, "Righteousness exalts a nation, but sin is a reproach to any people." There is no victory without righteousness.

The Gospel of Peace

The fourth weapon is having your feet fitted with the readiness of the gospel of peace. Proclaiming the gospel is one of the greatest spiritual weapons we have. We need to be moving from one city to another, proclaiming the good news, the Kingdom of God. Romans 10.15 says, "And how shall they preach unless they are sent? As it is written: 'How beautiful are the feet of those who preach the gospel of peace, who bring glad tidings of good things!'" God protects those who go about spreading the gospel of the Kingdom of God, bringing good news to those who are in despair.

The Sheild of Faith

The fifth weapon in our spiritual armor is the shield of faith. Faith is what connects us to God. It is like Wi-Fi—we cannot see it, but we see its effect when it works. As Hebrews 11.6 tells us, "But without faith it is impossible to please Him, for he who comes to God must believe that He is, and that He is a rewarder of those who diligently seek Him." Of all the Christian virtues, faith honours God the most. Our walk as Christians is a walk of faith, not based on what we see with our eyes, but on what we believe in our hearts. God responds to faith and nothing else; it is faith that moves Him.

Faith is also our shield, offering protection against Satan's fiery darts of doubt and anxiety. Satan's most powerful and seductive weapon is doubt. Doubt, like a seed, grows when it is planted in the heart and can disrupt our thoughts and undermine our trust in God. Doubt has led many believers into collision with God, as doubt offends Him, undermines our relationship with Him and distorts our understanding of who He is and what He is capable of doing. A heart filled with doubt becomes a home for the devil.

As a born-again Christian, you must guard your heart against nurturing seeds of doubt. James 1.6-8 warns us: "But let him ask in faith, with no doubting, for he who doubts is like a wave of the sea driven and tossed by the wind. For let not that man suppose that he will receive anything from the Lord; he is a double-minded man, unstable in all his ways." Doubt makes us unstable and hinders our ability to receive anything from God. Therefore, we must hold firm to the shield of faith, using it to protect our hearts from doubt and to stand strong in our relationship with God.

The Helmet of Salvation

The sixth weapon, which the Lord in His manifold wisdom has made available to the believer, is the helmet of salvation. How does this weapon work, and how important is it in the battle against Satan and his schemes? Your mind must fully believe this: that God has saved you through the death and resurrection of His Son, Jesus Christ. In life, many things happen, many mistakes we make, and many gaps we create because we live in the Adamic nature. Our minds are left wandering a great deal, asking questions like: Am I truly saved? Am I believing a lie? How can God accept me after all I've done?

It reminds me of a story. In 2004, I took a train from Birmingham, heading to Wales with a friend for a business meeting. We were on fire for God and found no shame in witnessing about Christ anywhere to anyone. We were nicely dressed, and as we glided into the journey, we started witnessing on the train. Many of our fellow travellers were astonished to see and hear us talk about Jesus and his saving grace. I started talking to one white man who was stone drunk. He told me that Jesus had nothing to do with a sinner like him. He confessed right there that he had murdered many people in South Africa and that Jesus could not love a man like him. I ministered to him and assured him that there is no sin Jesus cannot forgive and that if he accepted Jesus right there, he would be saved. He did.

I laid hands on him in the train, and immediately, the power of God touched and transformed him. He burst into laughter and tears—tears of joy. He became sober and clung to me, saying, "I don't know what to do. I was going to drink with my friends, but after you prayed, I have no desire for alcohol anymore." Friends, this is what salvation offers: a new life, free from condemnation and doubt. Our minds are sanctified and cleansed to think on things that are pure, lovely, and of good report (Phil. 4.8). Salvation, the eternal grace of God, has the power to protect our minds from the arrows of self-doubt and self-deception to believe that God saves absolutely through our faith of what Christ did on the cross. Believe you are saved, for you are indeed saved—not by your works, but by the gift of God in Christ Jesus (Eph. 2.8-9).

The Sword of the Spirit

The last weapon we can use is the sword of the Spirit, which is the word of God. As Hebrews 4.12-13 tells us, "For the word of God is living and powerful, and sharper than any two-edged sword, piercing even to the division of soul and spirit, and of joints and marrow, and is a discerner of the thoughts and intents of the heart. And there is no creature hidden from His sight, but all things are naked and open to the eyes of Him to whom we must give account." This scripture describes the potent power in the word of God. The devil fears the word of God. Jesus, in His temptation in the wilderness, defeated the devil by saying, "It is written" (Matt. 4.4). Jesus meant it is written in the word of God. The devil, your adversary, trembles at the mention of the word of God.

The Bible tells us that Jesus Christ is the word of God that became flesh (John 1.14). At the mention of Jesus, the Word of God, every knee shall bow, and every tongue will confess that Jesus Christ is Lord (Phil. 2.10-11). The centurion said to Jesus, "Just speak the word" (Matt. 8.8). The word of God has tremendous power to change absolutely anything when it is spoken from a heart full of faith. Do not allow your tongue to speak what does not come from the Lord our God.

Now you have come to understand the battle and the spiritual tools you need to use to fight this battle. It's time for you to listen carefully and to read this last part with caution. Read it prayerfully.

I want you to get this: it's not just about fighting the battle, but much more about how you fight the battle. It is good to know that you cannot just sit and expect things to change—you have to do something. "Faith without works is dead" (Jas 2.26). There is no gain without labour. There is work you have to do in order to achieve your goal. Your goal must be to bring an end to the embarrassment of suffering defeat all the time. This is what I have termed the **cycle of defeat.** It's a cycle because it repeats itself, 360 degrees, 365 days a year. Your life is constantly plagued by this negative experience. But what if I were to tell you today that it is possible to end this pattern in your life? How would you feel? I want you to know that this is not a mere suggestion—it is the will of God for you in Christ Jesus. God has made you more than a conqueror (Rom. 8.37). God has a good plan for you (Jer. 29.11). All you need to do is walk into the plan of God. Yet many people choose a painful path. Somehow, we miss the mark and choose to walk out of God's plan. This is the devil's deception, suggesting we can invent another way. Jesus is the way and it is settled (John 14:6). You do not need to Google and figure out things. He has already figured it out for you. This is the wisdom you need. Live it out, and you will be a winner.

But how do you fight? I want you to know it's not by might nor by power, but by the Spirit of God (Zech. 4.6). Gird the loins of your mind for battle. Be courageous and believe that God is fighting the battle for you, because God indeed is fighting for you without a shadow of a doubt. You need to lay hold of the promises of God in His Word. Meditate on the Word and speak it out. You receive what you meditate on and what you speak out. In the Word of God, we find life—true and meaningful life—that is freely offered to us by God. "This Book of the Law shall not depart from your mouth, but you shall meditate in it day and night, that you may observe to do according to all that is written in it. For then you will make your way prosperous, and then you will have good success" (Josh. 1.8). It is important that we meditate on the Word of God daily. We don't do it one day and then do something else another day—no, absolutely not! Each day, we must meditate on the Word and confess what it says about our situation. By doing this, you are fighting, and the cycle of defeat is being broken. You don't just need to meditate; make sure you are careful to observe everything written in the Word and to obey it. Obedience is the master key.

By holding fast to the Word, Esther changed the course of Israel's history. Daniel changed the Babylonian Empire. Joseph became the prime minister of Egypt. Moses delivered the children of Israel from bondage after 430 years. I can assure you that your interaction and communion with the Word of God is one of the most powerful and remarkable experiences you will ever have in your life. You're standing now at the threshold of history. You are about to be a history-maker. Your faith and focus will break the constant cycle of defeat. God has guaranteed your victory. Now, I say to you, step out in faith. The battle belongs to God, and the victory belongs to you. I can see you coming out with a testimony Do not hesitate to act on the Word of God. Do not delay, do not waste time. God is a God of the NOW. *Now is the time. Now is the day of deliverance. Now is the moment of redemption. Now is the time to act and activate the promises of God.* Your attitude and mindset will determine how long you will have to fight. Reset your mind now, and you will see immediate results.

At the right time, Jesus Christ called out Lazarus from the grave, and the dead situation came to life (John 11.43-44). Ezekiel spoke the word of God with the backing of God, and the valley of dry bones became the plateau of success (Ezek. 37.1-10). Paul and Silas praised God in the midst of the prison, and suddenly an earthquake broke their chains (Acts 16.25-26). Did you know that God wants to end the tyranny of failure and defeat in your life? God wants to change your story. God is turning your trials into triumphs, your setbacks into breakthroughs, and your limitations into limitless possibilities for your future. I can see that as you're reading this book, change is already happening. God says, "Forget the former things; do not dwell on the past. See, I am doing a new thing" (Isa. 43.18-19). Many people are in a prison of past experiences and cannot see beyond their situation. But as for you, your story is different. I see you coming out of that valley of defeat. I see you wearing a victor's crown. Shout for joy, for the Lord has done it for you!

THE SECRET OF BREAKING THE CYCLE OF DEFEAT | 45

I want to share more with you. Are you ready to hear the unexpected? Before I share this, I want to prepare you for it and I will return to where we started. Let me sum up the key points:

1. Know the battle you are fighting; it pays to spend time defining the battle.
2. Know the reason why you are fighting the battle. Your fighting must have a purpose.
3. Choose your battles wisely.
4. God defines and hand-picks the weapons you fight with in your battle.
5. The battle belongs to God, and you are just a medium.
6. Be focused and courageous. God cannot use a discouraged servant.
7. Know that you are a winner and more than a conqueror.
8. You are of a royal priesthood, totally peculiar—never doubt it.
9. Believe the promises, confess the Word, and you will have a revolution through revelation.
10. Never speak words that make Satan think he is winning.

Victory is not merely the outcome of a battle; it is a mindset formed before the battle is even fought. If I do not reset my mind before entering the battle, no matter how hard I fight, defeat is certain. One cannot win a battle with a defeated mindset. A defeated mindset will inevitably lead to defeat, no matter how hard one may fight. Take a moment to reflect—a serious reflection—and reset your mind. Your heart has to lead your mind in what you are believing God for before you engage in the battle.

Many people make the mistake of entering a battle with an undecided mind. Their mind is wandering, unsure whether they should fight or not, whether they will win or not, or whether this battle is even for them. Double-mindedness is the symptom of failure. It is like a seed that has been roasted; no matter how much you nurture it, it is a dead seed and will not bring life to you. We must be cautious of double-mindedness, for this is the very thing the devil will quickly offer us during times of temptation and trials. Doubt often speaks louder than faith.

Have you ever encountered a loud person? When they enter a room, they speak so loudly that you are tempted to believe they are the only person present, even though others are in the room. This is how doubt works—it often speaks and projects itself in your mind as if it is the only option that is available to you. It seductively tells you that doubt is the ONLY OPTION available. On the other hand, faith is like a quiet person—quiet—but when given the opportunity, faith does not just speak; it speaks with tremendous results. It is important to allow this quiet gentleman, faith, to speak and take charge of your heart, so that your heart can direct your mind.

Many people have missed it in life because they gave room to doubt and its cousin, double-mindedness. When these two come together, they ruin the party. You must closely watch them, as they are destiny spoilers. They must never be allowed to operate in any area of a believer's life. You must keep these two in check so that they cannot ruin your destiny and the plan God has for you.

God has given me the gift of insight and revelation, and sometimes I am amazed by how much we miss things and how much we resist that which God has provided for our redemption. We often laugh at what God is saying to us. When God said to Abraham, "This time next year, Sarah your wife shall have a son," Sarah laughed, and she laughed hard (Gen. 18.10-12). The angel was upset with her attitude and utter unbelief. Sarah had been in the cycle of barrenness for years, and it seemed the reality— she couldn't imagine that it could come to an end. She laughed at what God was saying, how foolish she was in the midst of her despair.

Do you laugh when you're told that your life will change for the better? Do you think it is hearsay? God proved Sarah wrong, and He fulfilled His promise to Abraham. Likewise, God's promises to you will be fulfilled as you act on His word.

Do not despair—there is no room for despair in an environment filled with the Word of God. God changes despair into hope, and He changes hope into the reality of celebration and victory. Now you will be changed by the promises of God. What you least expect will become the outcome of your destiny. You will become the testimony everyone will be talking about in the city.

It only takes faith in the Word of God. As you read this book, take a moment to pause—breathe in and out—and just wait and see what the Lord will do for you.

5

The Three Master Keys

Do not forget this! Never lose sight of this very important fact: God wants you to break the cycle of defeat. This is God's will for you. It can sometimes be difficult to believe, especially when you have missed the mark many times. We often drift into self-condemnation and self-righteousness. However, I have come to realize that no matter how hard I work, my work counts for nothing; it is the grace of God that will take me there. You may say, "then, let's continue sinning because whatever we do cannot contribute to our salvation." This is the deception many Christians fall into, believing that because of grace, they can be reckless and assume grace will redeem them. This is not the mindset of someone who is truly born again.

Paul at one point asked the same question, ""Shall we continue in sin that grace may abound?" (Rom. 6.1). Paul answered with an emphatic no. Let's look at the Scripture for the benefit of those unfamiliar with it:

What shall we say then? Shall we continue in sin that grace may abound? Certainly not! How shall we who died to sin live any longer in it? Or do you not know that as many of us as were baptized into Christ Jesus were baptized into His death? Therefore we were buried with Him through baptism into death, that just as Christ was raised from the dead by the glory of the Father, even so we also should walk in newness of life (Rom. 6.1-4).

God has offered us a new life, and this new life is not connected to the cycle of defeat. In this new life defeat has been done away with. It is the old life, that is connected to the cycle of defeat. It is the old life that is connected to past hurts and disappointment. But thanks be to God, who does not want to see those who belong to him bound in prison of their old life. Through the death of Christ on the cross, a new picture emerges—a picture of great possibilities. In this new picture, an ordinary believer with no education or good background has an equal chance as a PhD graduate or a university professor. This is the beauty of God's love. God does not anoint titles or diplomas; He anoints one's character. It is in your character that God will reside or abide. You cannot obtain character from a Bible college or university. You can learn about character in these places, but you can't develop character through a diploma. Character is the work one does on oneself; it is a deep cleansing and aligning of oneself to the nature and character of God. It is the radical change that happens to those who allow the Holy Spirit to work on their nature.

You must be determined to fashion your life in conformity with the life of Christ. Character is everything—it is the master key to unlocking the realms of possibilities in your destiny. If you want true victory, work on your character. Put forth the greatest effort to uproot the weeds that try to suffocate your life. Satan uses the small foxes to spoil our vine that is blossoming. He is the spoiler of destinies, using our weaknesses to fight us. He is a skilled taskmaster who seduces and plots the downfall and failure of great people.

But as a born-again believer, you do not need to fear Satan. 1 Peter 5.8 says, "Your adversary the devil walks about like a roaring lion, seeking whom he may devour." Notice carefully: Satan is not a lion—he only roars like one. He is a counterfeit, attempting to intimidate you. Jesus Christ is the true Lion of the tribe of Judah.

In the battle against the cycle of defeat, there are three keys we need to discuss in this chapter. These are keys that are often overlooked, yet they are profound and powerful principles and secrets that a believer must learn and acquire to defeat the cycle of defeat.

The incredible power of the virtue of consistency.

THE SECRET OF BREAKING THE CYCLE OF DEFEAT | 51

Consistency is an incredible key—it is the power behind the throne of victory. There is no way one can succeed in life without practicing the virtue of consistency. Consistency is a potent habit, a person's lethal weapon against defeat and failure. Before anyone can experience success, they must learn the principle of consistency. But what does it mean?

We often hear about consistency, but what does it truly mean? Consistency is the discipline of repeating something over and over again until its real value is unlocked. It is the act of repeating an activity until it produces results. We do not stop until the activity produces results. Most things in life will not work on the first try. It is through repetition that their best potential is realized.

To be consistent, you require real discipline. "You cannot be a winner without maturity and consistency. With consistency, repetition, and routine, you will achieve your goals and get where you want to be. Trust is built with consistency" (Silva, Roose, and Chafee). Maya Angelou also said, "One is not born with courage, but one is born with potential. Without courage, we cannot practice any other virtue with consistency." Nothing works unless one is consistent. Nothing shines unless it is polished consistently.

A silversmith must keep polishing metal until its beauty and strength are revealed. A farmer must consistently nurture the seed until it produces a harvest. A mother must feed her child repeatedly for that child to grow into an adult. This practice must be done over and over again until faith becomes real and living. Marriages reach maturity and success when love is consistently given.

Nothing works until you learn the value of consistency. Many people have failed and been defeated because they tried once or twice and then stopped. However, you can be a wonder by practicing the virtue of consistency.

Are you consistent in what you do? What stops or discourages you? Every small act, repeated, has the potential to grow into something incredibly big. Dreams may start small, but it is in repeating them that their true potential is revealed.

Consistency is like the foundation of a building; without it, you cannot build or sustain anything. Nothing; no dream, effort or action becomes meaningful until consistency comes into the picture. Consistency is the fact check for success—it has to be present for anyone to articulate the concept of success. But the pressing question is, how do you build consistency or how does one become consistent?

Does consistency simply come about? Absolutely not. Consistency is a habit, defined as a "settled practice" or, as the Britannica Dictionary states, "a usual way of behaving, something that a person does often in a regular and repeated way." It must be pursued with the sole intention of achieving success. It takes discipline and principle to develop a good habit. Unfortunately, many destinies today are destroyed because people in the 21st century see little value in discipline and principle. Yet success is hidden in these two pillars.

Consistency is born out of practice. We must practice, and do so consistently—continuously, repeatedly—until we see results. Some call this principle by the acronym P.U.S.H.—Pray Until Something Happens. The problem is that many pray but stop before something happens. Many people can start something, but they are not patient enough to wait to see the results. Isaiah 40.31 reminds us, "But those who wait on the Lord shall renew their strength; they shall mount up with wings like eagles, they shall run and not be weary, they shall walk and not faint."

Our generation is interested in shortcuts and quick fixes. We seem saturated with the Microwave Philosophy, where everything must happen instantly. However, success requires stepping out of comfort zones, pushing more, pressing harder, persevering, and maintaining determination. By so doing, these habits give birth to the virtue of consistency. When consistency has fully matured, the opportunities and possibilities are endless. The sky becomes the limit and the horizon expand. So, in every activity and action, build the virtue of consistency, and you will breathe life into your destiny.

Consistency is like oxygen to the body—without it, there is no life. You cannot break the strongholds of the cycle of defeat unless you develop the habit of consistency in at least three key areas of your life.

Consistency in Prayer

The power of prayer is often talked about, yet many Christians do not know how to use prayer as a leverage to unlock and release their life from the cycle of defeat. The songwriter says, "Oh, what peace we often forfeit, oh, what needless pain we bear, all because we do not carry everything to God in prayer." "Pray, I am praying for you, say a prayer for me" are common words and words spoken more often yet less understood by those who use it. Prayer is frequently misunderstood, mishandled, or treated lightly by those who attempt to engage in it. However, Prayer is a weapon, it is a hammer in the mouth of a believer that can be used to break the cycle of defeat. I have come to understand that prayer is the most powerful spiritual activity; whose power, effect and impact on human life is often underestimated. Why is it so?

There are certain philosophical principles that undermine prayer, which most believers are not accustomed to, not aware of or that they rarely understand. Prayer is often seen as a lofty, complex spiritual activity, seemingly reserved for great masters and theologians. Yet prayer, in its simplest form, is a conversation —a simple dialogue between humanity and divinity. It does not have to be clustered by religious phraseology of spirituality—when man may seem to some extent important and spiritual.

I insist that prayer is a conversation, a simple conversation between man and God. One does not need to use religious jargon to engage effectively in prayer. It is an honest talk between man and God. I remember, after years of struggling with alcohol, I made one of the simplest yet most important prayers that changed my life. I lifted my hands in the air and said, "Jesus, if you are there, help me to break the habit of drinking alcohol. I cannot help myself." It was just that simple. That night, God responded to my prayer and broke the chains of alcoholism—without a preacher. God set me free. I have been free since, never again have I been tempted be alcohol.

Did I pray a complicated prayer? No. Absolutely not. The truth is that humanity has missed it—prayer is a sincere conversation that must be done consistently. Two things matter in prayer: sincerity and consistency. These are the ingredients of true prayer that God answers.

Consistency in Church Attendance

Just like prayer, church attendance is often misconstrued and misunderstood. Many people come to church when they want or when it fits their schedule. Church attendance to them is a luxury. Yet to those who are deeply spiritual, church attendance is an absolute necessity that can only bear fruit if it is done in an orderly and consistent fashion.

How is your church attendance? Do you attend only sporadically, maybe once a month? Why is your church attendance erratic, inconsistent and at best, haphazard? It's because you do not understand the spiritual value of church attendance.

In the early church, people attended church daily (Acts 2.46). Church attendance was never a one-day event, as seen in the 21st century. It was always a daily thing or a daily activity. Church attendance helps to build our faith and strengthen our relationship with God. Without it, we are Christians without strength and hope. The more like-minded people gather together consistently, the more a radical and wonderful atmosphere is created, which is a leverage for breaking the cycle of defeat. Unfortunately, the decline in church attendance has seen the rise in human failure and cycles of defeat. The only way we can counteract human failure and defeat is to capsulate church attendance—to energize and supercharge our spiritual life and beat the gates of the cycle of defeat for the glory of God.

Make every effort to be deliberate and intentional. Make time to attend church, as simple as it may seem. Take it seriously. Plan for it and create a schedule. You will be amazed by how much you can achieve. Ask yourself this question: Why am I going to church? What do I want to achieve? Doing so helps you listen to the message with purpose and clarity. Your presence in church will find meaning and purpose, allowing you to grow, mature, and become more productive.

Since I became born again, I have consistently attended church, and I have done so strategically. It has helped shape my spiritual life in profound ways. I have seen an increase in knowledge, wisdom and the capacity to resolve challenges I have encountered and calm many storms that have threatened to sink my life. When attending church, don't be anxious or religious; aim to be spiritual and productive. Many pastors spend countless hours researching and preparing sermons, and if we would take those messages seriously, the possibilities for growth and transformation are limitless.

Consistence in Obedience
"Obedience is better than sacrifice" (1 Sam. 15.22).

We live in a free world and today, to be free seems to suggest that "you can do what you want, when you want." Look at the Nike goal, "Just Do It," suggesting that life is a blank check. However, life requires some principles and guidelines. Paul warns us in 2 Timothy 3.1-5 about the challenges of the last days:

"But know this, that in the last days perilous times will come: For men will be lovers of themselves, lovers of money, boasters, proud, blasphemers, disobedient to parents, unthankful, unholy, unloving, unforgiving, slanderers, without self-control, brutal, despisers of good, traitors, headstrong, haughty, lovers of pleasure rather than lovers of God, having a form of godliness but denying its power. And from such people turn away!" (2 Tim.3.1-5)

Life must be lived on both principle and purpose. Christians have a greater duty and responsibility to order their lives in a way that glorifies God, both in how they live and in what they live for. From Genesis to Revelation, we see humanity's repeated failure—particularly the failure to obey God's instructions.

In the Garden of Eden, Adam was told not to eat the fruit from the tree of life. It was a simple instruction, but it contained the very secret between life and death, between failure and success. Humanity's depraved condition is reflected throughout the pages of the Bible. What we see clearly is the contrast between those who are obedient and those who are disobedient. It is a state of the Cost of disobedience and the consequences that are attended to it. The pain and the hurts disobedience has brought to humanity are evident through history. For example, Saul was given a clear instruction to completely destroy the Amalekites. By modifying this command, he wrecked his destiny (1 Sam. 15.3-23). Similarly, Moses missed the honour of entering the Promised Land due to a single act of disobedience (Num. 20.12). Samson, too, destroyed a great destiny through his disobedience (Judg. 16.20). God wants us to obey, for in obedience we demonstrate our trust and loyalty to Him. Yet, humanity prefers shortcuts, even though we know that shortcuts often turn out to be the longest route to the end of the matter.

One cannot obey unless one's heart is totally yielded to God. It is not obedience one day, but obedience all the time. Obedience must never be an event; it must be a lifestyle of one who truly believes and trusts God. Obedience is the only measure of the truth, sincerity and genuineness of a person. I will never know who you are unless I can see your obedience at work in a consistent lifestyle. Greatness needs a key to unlock it, and it seems to me without a shadow of doubt, that obedience is the real key to greatness and success.

Obedience will no doubt help you to break the cycle of defeat and usher your destiny into the realm of possibilities and opportunity. Nothing will work unless obedience is attached to the conduct or behaviour of the one doing it. Every military commander knows that unless his soldiers are obedient, he can kiss his dream of victory goodbye. Nowhere than in the military is the value of obedience clearly articulated and illuminated.

How do you view obedience? How often are you obedient? Does it matter to you? There are certain principles you can't do without. These are principles that Encapsulate human life. Obedience is one said principle. It is a concept and Principle one cannot do away with. Success screams loud and clear: "I cannot do it without my cousin, Obedience." Learn and apply it and the outlook is totally different. This is a master key to breaking the cycle of defeat.

6

The Temptation to Forget

Now that you have come this far, I want to remind you that you did not do it by yourself. God has been the power behind the throne of your victory. The victory you wish to enjoy—or perhaps already enjoy—is made possible by God and God alone. While this may seem obvious and simple, it is important to make things simple without allowing Simplicity to overtake them. Simplicity should not diminish the depth of significance. There is a difference between simplicity and being simple. Simplicity often breeds contempt. Making things simple may help us to understand them, but when we allow simplicity to enter into the simple things we are doing, we can easily allow the spirit of familiarity to destroy sacred things.

Many Christians today have allowed simplicity and familiarity to destroy things that are sacred. We must never make things that are holy, unholy. As Jesus warned, "Do not cast your pearls before swine" (Matt. 7.6). This is the greatest tragedy the modern church is facing —a real spiritual threat of great proportion. It must never be taken for granted, lest, it destroys what God is doing. The prophet Ezekiel warned: "Her priests have violated My law and profaned My holy things; they have not distinguished between the holy and the unholy, nor have they made known the difference between the unclean and the clean; and they have hidden their eyes from My Sabbaths so that I am profaned among them" (Ezek. 22.26).

Many Christians have violated the principle of separating holy things from unholy things. How can one break the cycle of defeat unless they learn to separate the holy from the unholy, the common from the uncommon, the great from the ordinary, and important matters from trivial ones? You see, here lies the greatest spiritual danger of humanity.

When Solomon was crowned king, his first important prayer was, "Lord, give me a discerning heart so that I may distinguish between good and evil" (1 Kings 3.9). How could the king rule? How could he administer justice and lead his people unless he understood the spiritual primacy, that is, the difference between good and evil? That difference is like day and night, yet in the midst of the two values lies the mystery of life. Those who want success and victory ought to carefully study and understand this principle. It is a spiritual law that cannot be violated and must be understood by anyone striving to reach the zenith of their destiny during the course of their human life. This principle forms the foundation that all who are called to greatness must embrace and obey.

There is no success without discipline, no discipline without training, no meaningful training without commitment, and one cannot commit and be loyal to a cause unless they are born again. Being born again brings a new, radical spiritual experience that awakens the spirit and ushers the individual into a realm of great possibilities. Do not limit yourself. To discover who you truly are, you must look to the Lord. This is the only option available: "Looking unto Jesus, the author and finisher of your faith" (Heb. 12.2).

Our eyes must focus on Him—on the One who was crucified, died, and was buried, and yet rose from the dead to give us new life. This new life is full of victory, possibilities, and purpose. A new life where He fills himself with himself into your life.

Are you born again? How strong is your connection with God? The stronger the connection, the greater the illumination. As Christians who aspire to live a victorious life, we face many temptations daily, one of the greatest being the temptation to forget where we have come from. The temptation to forget where God has taken us from is the real weapon the devil uses, destroying the bridge between our past and our present so that we lose sight of where we are coming from. However, God reminds us to remember always where He has taken us from.

King David never forgot what the Lord had done for him. The psalmist declared in Psalms 116:12 "Because He has inclined His ear to me, therefore I will call upon Him as long as I live. The pains of death surrounded me, and the pangs of Sheol laid hold of me; I found trouble and sorrow." The Psalmist crafted his response very carefully:

1. He says, "I will take the cup of salvation and call upon the name of the Lord" (Ps. 116.13). This was a clear acknowledgment that it was not by his own strength, but God did it for him.
2. David continues, "I will pay my vows to the Lord now in the presence of all His people" (Ps. 116.14). Because he understood the enormity of God's grace and mercy, he was committed to paying his vows publicly, as a declaration of thanksgiving and praise. How often do we become shy and secretive when God has redeemed us? Do people know your testimony? Are you shy to say, "When I came to the Lord, I was like Naaman with leprosy, but now see what the Lord has done for me"? Or, do you say publicly, "When I came to the Lord, or when I came to the church, I was bleeding for many years like that woman who had an issue of blood, but the Lord Located me here"? Are you being forced to Share your testimony? David wasn't shy, he was inspired to share his testimony publicly. As a prophet of God, I can tell you that those who hide their testimony or hide the source of their victory, in most cases will not be able to maintain it. Have you ever seen a Christian who was redeemed by God at one point, only to find them in an even worse situation later? The simple, yet profound reason is that they forgot the source of their victory.
3. When David brought the Ark of the Lord to Jerusalem, he danced like a madman, before the Lord. His wife Michal, the

daughter of Saul, despised him for it. In 2 Samuel 6.20, she ridiculed him, saying, "How glorious was the king of Israel today, uncovering himself today in the eyes of the maids of his servants, as one of the base fellows shamelessly uncovers himself!" David's response was profound: "It was before the Lord, who chose me instead of your father and all his house, to appoint me ruler over the people of the Lord, over Israel. Therefore, I will play music before the Lord. And I will be even more undignified than this, and will be humble in my own sight. But as for the maidservants of whom you have spoken, by them I will be held in honor" (2 Sam. 6.21–22). David knew that his greatness, influence, and might came solely from God. It was clear to David that it was the Lord who had made him king, and it was not a trivial thing. As a result, he had to pay homage to God who had Lifted him up.

Many Christians have forgotten who lifted them up, treating their place of redemption and victory with disdain and dishonour. No wonder their lives seem cursed by the Lord. Samuel concluded that because Michal took lightly what God had done for David, she forgot that it was the Lord who had made her queen through making David king. How could she lightly esteem the Lord and easily forget what the Lord had done to lift her up through the promotion of her husband David? We are told. "And Michal, the daughter of Saul, had no child to the day of her death" (2 Sam. 6.23).

Have you talked and sabotaged yourself by becoming drunk with success and victory, forgetting how you arrived at your place of pre-eminence? Are you despising the very place that lifted you up? Do you despise your parents or your friends who stood with you at the time when you were in the valley? Have you forgotten the pastor who stood with you in your desperate and loneliest moments? Are you now ashamed to be identified with those who stood with you at your darkest hour? How do you treat those who were with you at the time of shame and leprose? Look back and see how you have treated the people who helped you in the past. Do you still maintain the same relationships you had during those difficult times? Do you respect and honour them as you once did? Have you been tempted by the devil to magnify their weaknesses, or have you allowed the devil to help you treat them with contempt?

How is it at that, at your darkest hour, you treated them like angels, and in the moment of your victory, you treat them as the devil incarnate? Humanity has fallen over and over again into the vicious cycle of defeat because of this tendency to easily forget. This is the strategy of the devil to keep Christians trapped in the cage of defeat and disappointment. To break free, you will have to change your mindset and your approach; otherwise, Satan will lock you up in an endless cycle of defeat. However, God has a plan for you—that you ought to break the cycle of defeat and be the person that the Lord has called you to be. Gratitude and thanksgiving are master keys that unlock destinies and spiritual horizons. Practice them, and you will experience the overflowing joy of living a victorious life filled with endless possibilities.

God commanded the children of Israel to take twelve stones and build a memorial to remember His faithfulness: "Lest you forget" (Josh. 4.7). This a reminder of the faithfulness of God. What do you keep as a reminder to the things God has done for you? Can you look back into your life and have vivid memories of what God has done for you? Do you have a spiritual "hard drive" where you store images of your milestones to reflect on occasionally? Anyone who wants to be victorious and end the cycle of defeat must learn the art and the mystery of the power of thanksgiving and praise. As the psalmist writes in Psalm 116.17, "I will offer to You the sacrifice of thanksgiving, and will call upon the name of the Lord."

There are moments in my life that I cannot just forget, regardless of my successes. I still have vivid memories of my beloved father cycling to work, back and forth, to give us a good education. Although my father has passed away, I cannot just erase those memories of a hero, fully determined to give his family the best life possible, in the most difficult circumstances. No amount of offense, hurt, or disappointment should make you forget where you came from. As the psalmist says in Psalms 11.3, "If the foundations be destroyed, what can the righteous do?" Forgetting where we came from is like destroying the foundation upon which our lives are built. When we destroy that foundation, what can we build? How can we build?

Memories must be handled with the greatest care and candor. The devil often manipulates and twists our memories to confuse and cage us in the cycle of defeat. What gave David the courage to fight Goliath and defeat him, is he remembered that God had rescued him from the Lion and the bear. The words of David are carefully recorded by the Prophet Samuel in 1 Samuel 17. 37 "Moreover, David said, 'The Lord, who delivered me from the paw of the lion and from the paw of the bear, He will deliver me from the hand of this Philistine.'" Saul responded, "Go, and the Lord be with you!"

For David, the God of yesterday secures his victory today and guarantees his victory tomorrow. There is great power in reminding oneself of what God has done in the past. How wonderful and beautiful are the memories of God's faithfulness, yet how often we conveniently forget. The devil is a master manipulator and deceptor. I have seen couples destroy their marriages because of one night of disagreement, with the devil turning that moment into a lifetime of resentment and pain. You will hear people say, "There is nothing you have ever done for me. Our life has always been hell. I have suffered all my life; I have never enjoyed this marriage," and the list is endless. The devil would have you remember one night of disagreement and make you forget the moments of joy and synergy that had kept you together.

The devil exaggerates and magnifies to deceive and manipulate. How often do we remember our mother's beatings rather than the sacrifices they made for our life? How do we conveniently remember our pastors' rebukes and corrections and forget their endless nights of travailing in prayer for us? This is the devil's strategy: to make us remember the negative and forget the positive, keeping us locked in cycles of defeat. Many people, unaware of the devil's strategy, have played into his trap.

A lot of people have been healed and blessed through my ministry, yet 90% of them have forgotten how they came to the church and the many sleepless nights I spent praying and fasting for them. They have forgotten how I stood in the gap for them between life and death. Consequently, the majority of them fall back into the same cycle of defeat because they forget the God of yesterday. While many have been blessed through this ministry, only 10% of them attribute their success to this place or the ministry God has given me. This pattern repeats itself, leading to setbacks. It seems the more we forget, the more power we give to the devil.

Our memories serve as anchors in times of temptation and trials. There is always another temptation: the temptation of failing to let go of past hurts and disappointments. The temptation to keep yesterday's failure alive and living is real, but God demands that we forget our past hurts and disappointments, in order to break the cycle of defeat and failure. In Isaiah 43.18–21, God says, "Do not remember the former things, nor consider the things of old. Behold, I will do a new thing; now it shall spring forth; shall you not know it? I will even make a road in the wilderness and rivers in the desert. The beasts of the field will honour Me, the jackals and the ostriches, because I give waters in the wilderness and rivers in the desert, to give drink to My people, My chosen. This people I have formed for Myself; they shall declare My praise. God wants us to let go of the poison of yesterday and hold on to the beautiful memories and possibilities of the future. Yet, many Christians prefer to hold on to bitterness, anger, and past hurts and disappointments instead of embracing the hope Christ offers.

David remembered the past kindness of Jonathan instead of the betrayal of Saul. Ruth chose to believe in the unseen future rather than hold on to the bitter memories of widowhood. Daniel chose to remember how the Lord rescued him from the den of lions rather than capitulate to the fear of the fiery furnace. Joseph forgot the betrayal of Potiphar's wife and the hatred and jealousy of his brothers, to hold on to the forgiveness and the endless possibilities of reconciliation that ultimately made him the Prime Minister of Egypt.

You see, your memories can either make you bitter or better. The choice is yours. God has given us the gift of free will, but I urge you to choose wisely. Joshua and Caleb chose to have faith in the Word of God rather than the fear imposed by the stature of their enemies. Their fellow countrymen said they felt like grasshoppers, yet Joshua and Caleb declared, "We can take over the land" (Num. 13.33; 14.9). You see, a little faith, like a mustard seed, is more powerful than a mountain of doubt. (Matt. 17.20).

Remembering your memories and your attitude of thanksgiving and gratitude is a potent weapon against the cycle of defeat and failure. The women who had been healed and delivered by Jesus partnered with Him because they remembered what He had done for them. "Now it came to pass, afterward, that He went through every city and village, preaching and bringing the glad tidings of the kingdom of God. And the twelve were with Him, and certain women who had been healed of evil spirits and infirmities—Mary called Magdalene, out of whom had come seven demons, and Joanna the wife of Chuza, Herod's steward, and Susanna, and many others who provided for Him from their substance" (Luke 8. 1-3). One leper returned to thank Jesus, prompting Him to ask, "Where are the nine? Why is it only one returning to give thanks?" (Luke 17.17-18). Are you among the nine, or do you identify with the one leper who returned to offer thanks?

How about Hannah, who chose to forgive the insult of Eli, "You are drunk," and instead remember the blessing, "Go your way; may the Lord grant you your request" (1 Sam. 1.14, 17). How often has your life been ruined because you chose to remember the bad instead of the good? Life is like art; where you focus will determine the beauty you see or the pain you remember. Many Christians mishandle their pain and their pasts, faltering because they forget where they are coming from.

Do you remember where you came from? Do you remember how God picked you up, dusted you off and turned your life around? The songwriter reminds us, "When I remember what the Lord has done, I will not turn back any more." Your memories are a lethal weapon against the cycle of defeat, and your thanksgiving is an armor meant to break the cycle of defeat. Your life is in your hands, but it is directed by God, the architect and creator of your life. In Him, victory is certain.

As you strive to wrestle with and break the cycle of defeat, it is important to reflect and do so soberly. Sobriety is the antidote to failure. It allows you the calmness that is required in moments of decision-making. Many people often make serious errors because they made their decisions in the heat of the moment—it was a rushed decision and it spoiled everything.

As I conclude this part of the book, I urge you to reflect and think soberly. Gratitude is a weapon often undermined by many Christians, yet it is one of the most effective weapons the Christian possesses. A grateful heart, filled with joy, is a wellspring of life (Prov.4.23). Practice to be thankful and take the practice of thanksgiving seriously. Let it become a lifestyle—something you will not want to miss or waste. Life is a mystery, requiring many keys to unlock its full potential. The cycle of defeat is like poison; it requires an antidote, and that antidote is thanksgiving.

I have witnessed gratitude work wonders, breaking barriers and strongholds. Now, you stand at a momentous occasion. Step out in faith and believe in God's Word. The cycle of defeat that has followed your life is melting like wax right now because of your faith in the

Word of God. It is changing the way you think and that will change the way you act. When you act the right way, the sky is the limit. I see you free from the entrapment or failure and setback. BELIEVE!

7

The Power Of Character

"Personality is an important thing. It is like a perfume. A spoken phrase, a look, an action or reaction, a gesture—any of these can reach a long way in memory or influence. A most stimulating book could be written on a banquet of saints in which the essence of a well-lived life would be distilled into a few pages for each. The Bible does it. Consider Esther or Ruth. A few paragraphs can capture the fragrance of a life and dispense it for centuries." (Showalter)

This is how we can capture the mystery and the power of character as I begin writing this chapter of this incredible and life-changing book. Handle its spiritual nuggets and gems well, and you will have made a worthwhile investment in your life.

You are now reading Chapter 6 of this very incredible book. It is a book, no doubt, that will change your life forever if you continue to read it carefully and study the principles set out in its blessed and sacred pages. It contains spiritual gems that will lift your destiny to greater heights. The book is well-thought-out and carefully crafted to give you the maximum advantage and insights in your fight against the cycle of defeat.

I can see that you have made up your mind to break the cycle of defeat and failure. You are sick and tired of living a life animated by setbacks and failure. I am glad that you are developing a mindset that will lead you to victory and success. Victory and success in the Christian life start with the Word of God. How you read the Bible and how you handle the Word of God will determine how well you understand your life and how well you will choose a spiritual path that will lead you to a spiritual experience that will change your destiny forever.

The Bible is not a book of literature, although it contains some aspects of literature. It is not a history book, though its pages contain important historical facts. It is not an economics book, though you will discover a corpus of economic knowledge within its pages. How you see and understand the Bible will determine how you read it and how you apply it to your life.

It must be understood that God will do nothing without His Word, for His Word is the seed that God uses to begin something new. Joshua, in the incredible book of Joshua, understood the importance of God's Word. He had learned many things from following Moses, the servant of God. In Joshua 1.8-9, he warned the people of Israel, writing a powerful instruction that we would do well to heed: "This Book of the Law shall not depart from your mouth, but you shall meditate in it day and night, that you may observe to do according to all that is written in it. For then you will make your way prosperous, and then you will have good success. Have I not commanded you? Be strong and of good courage; do not be afraid, nor be dismayed, for the Lord your God is with you wherever you go"

Meditation on God's Word brings us closer to Him, and the closer we are to God, the better the outcome of our lives. Do not regard the Bible as a mere book, for it is not an ordinary book. The Bible is, in essence, God Himself. This may sound strange or even wrong, but it is the unavoidable truth.

Let us look at the book of John. Perhaps you need to understand who John was—the man and apostle who wrote the Gospel of John. John had a unique relationship with Jesus Christ and held a special place in His inner circle. He was known as the beloved disciple of Jesus (John 13.23), the one who leaned on the bosom of Jesus and was trusted by Him. John was often set apart from the other twelve disciples. When Jesus was transfigured on the mountain, it was Peter, James, and John who were present, witnessing Jesus conversing with the ancient heroes of faith (Matt. 17.1-3). It was also John who stood by the cross when Jesus, entrusted His mother Mary into John's care, saying, "Woman, behold your son!" and to John, "Behold your mother!" (John 19.26-27). What profoundness in that rare and glorious moment at one of Jesus's critical stages of his human life.

John also wrote in the opening verses of his Gospel: "In the beginning was the Word, and the Word was with God, and the Word was God. He was in the beginning with God. All things were made through Him, and without Him nothing was made that was made. In Him was life, and the life was the light of men" (John 1.1-4).

Anyone who sits down to read the Bible sits down to have a conversation with God—a dialogue with the King of Kings and the Lord of Lords. God is literally present by His Word, and when one reads, one opens a conversation with Him. As I write, I feel the incredible presence of God all around me. Can you see God when you open the pages of the Bible? Many people make the mistake of reading the Bible like a novel, newspaper, or history book. No, you would be absolutely wrong. Read the Bible as a sacred conversation with God, and your life will never be the same again.

The Bible often seems "boring" to some because they have no clue what it is or how to approach this unique and sacred book. It is not merely a book; it is a person—the person of God, revealed and illuminated in its pages. You may ask, "Why are you saying all these things? The title of your chapter is The Power of Character in Breaking the Cycle of Defeat. Just tell me the secret. That's all I want to hear." But every secret has a foundation and origin. Unless the origin and foundation of the secret are well understood, the secret is often misunderstood, misapplied, or misconstrued. You see, our sentence is full of "mis" —indicating that we are missing something important that makes the secret or principle meaningful.

Character is very important, yet its significance and place in the fight against the cycle of defeat is not well understood or appreciated by many Christians. Often, when people talk about character, they pay lip service to it. However, in this book, I will show you how important character is and how you can use it to break the cycle of defeat and failure. God hates defeat and failure; He has not designed His creation to suffer defeat but to live in victory. Victory is God's crown, and He has crowned His children with the crown of victory to bring glory to His name. If you truly understand this, your attitude will change.

There are three keys associated with character, which I have termed the "Trinity of Victory." Many people do not understand the significance of the number three in Hebrew. Hebrew philosophy and knowledge carry profound mysteries about human life. We are told, "For where two or three are gathered together in My name, I am there in the midst of them" (Matt. 18.20), and "By the mouth of two or three witnesses every word shall be established" (2 Cor. 13.1). Ecclesiastes 4.12 tells us, "A cord of three strands is not easily broken."

What is the significance of number three? Why am I talking about the Trinity of victory? Why do I talk of the Trinity of faith? I will show you this in a moment. The "Trinity of Victory" consists of three imperatives and significant keys: character, attitude, and personality These three keys are crucial to breaking the cycle of defeat, but first things first. In Hebrew, the number three is "gimel," which signifies "divine fullness" or "perfection." It means "to be lifted up," and while pride is its negative aspect, its positive side represents being glorified or elevated to a position of authority. The number three reflects divine completeness and perfection.

Consider how often the number three appears in the Bible. God presents Himself as Father, Son, and Holy Spirit (Gen. 1.26). Noah had three sons (Gen. 6.10). Abraham welcomed three incredible visitors (Gen. 18.2). Jonah was in the belly of the fish for three years (Jonah 1.17). Jesus overcame Satan's temptations in the wilderness by quoting Scripture three times (Matt. 4.1-11). Jesus's earthly ministry was completed in three days, Peter denied Him three times (Luke 22.54-62), and Jesus questioned Peter three times to confirm his love (John 21.15-17). There is no doubt in my mind that the number three is a pattern and symbol of victory.

To fully understand the impact of character in breaking the cycle of defeat, we will have to see the three aspects or keys that really constitute character and that which can give a Christian power against the cycle of defeat.

Character + attitude + personality= Power or Victory.

When these three keys appear and are properly handled, they give a Christian significant power over the cycle of defeat. I will break down these important keys for you in this Part of the book so that you can understand them and then apply them to your life in the fight against the cycle of defeat and failure.

According to The Britannica Dictionary, character is "the way someone thinks, feels, and behaves: someone's personality—usually singular." However, to truly understand character, we must trace its Greek origin. The Greek word *charassein,* meaning "to sharpen, cut, or engrave," gives us the noun *character,* meaning a "mark" or "distinct quality" (Britannica). Merriam-Webster defines character traits as part of your behaviour, beliefs, and personality that help others understand who you are personally and professionally (Merriam-Webster). No doubt, your character plays a very important role in your fight against the cycle of defeat.

I often tell people that God does not anoint titles; He anoints character. Before God gives someone power and authority, He looks for character. Character is like a container—if it has holes, whatever is poured into it will be lost. In order for you to fight something, you need authority and power to do so, otherwise you will be fighting a losing battle. Jesus said to His disciples in Luke 10.19, "Behold, I give you the authority to trample on serpents and scorpions, and over all the power of the enemy, and nothing shall by any means hurt you."

Before Jesus gave power and authority, He had to look for character. He spent three years building the disciples' character so that they could be able to receive the anointing to fight against the schemes of the devil. Imagine if the disciples had not worked their character, what would have happened? With the story of Judas, we see how he failed to develop character and his failure led to moral failure which ruined his destiny. God wants us to reflect himself; His traits and qualities in order for us to fight against the cycle of defeat and break it.

It took Moses forty years to build the character that would qualify him to be a deliverer of Israel. Joseph went through the pit, prison and persecution to build his character so that he could be the Prime Minister of Egypt. Daniel went through the den of lions and the fiery furnace to build his character. Many Christians today lack character or have flawed characters because they refuse to have their character moulded. God often uses tests and trials to mould someone's Character.

Character is not something we are born with; it is made through the trenches and valleys of human life. What we go through shapes our character and ultimately determines our personality, how we present ourselves to others, and ultimately gives us the attitude we have. As the writer says, "Our attitude determines our altitude." We cannot climb the ladder of greatness in life unless we wake our character and attitude. Many gifted people have failed at the point of victory because their character and attitude let them down.

Be honest with yourself—does your character and attitude sometimes let you down? how many times has your character or attitude ruined an otherwise glorious opportunity for you? If truth is to be told, you have allowed your character many times to ruin the best of opportunities God has presented to you. A man's character is his fate. Character is that which reveals moral purpose, exposing the class of things a person chooses or avoids. Character to your destiny is like the heart to the human body—without it, there is no life. No meaningful progress and success can occur without a fortified character. If a man desires to be honest and achieve success in an honourable way, he has to spend a lot of time watching his character. As Robert Tow wisely stated, "Strength of character isn't always about how much you can handle before you break; it's also about how much you can handle after you have been broken." This speaks volumes about the importance of character Imperatives. Here lies the human life bridge that separates success and failure.

In Philippians 2.5 (AMPC) Paul instructs us to "Let this same attitude (Character) that was in Christ, be also in you." What character do we see in Jesus? What does the life of Jesus Christ reveal about his character? He was a man of principle, honesty, love, faith, moral fortitude and resilience, and deep knowledge and wisdom. The list is endless. Even though He was accused daily, no deceit was found in Him because He was a man of impeccable integrity and character. His character was a weapon, a wall of defence and shield against the arrows of the enemy.

If Jesus worked so hard to reflect a glorious character in His earthly and human life, how much more should you apply yourself to build an impeccable character—one that carries the fragrance of beauty and the strength of an arrow to fight the enemy in the cycle of defeat and failure? Character is what we become when we choose to tirelessly work on ourselves to refine and beautify our lives. The end result is not just beauty, but power, strength, and a force of fortitude that can destroy every barrier or negative cycle that seeks to animate our lives.

In true character, you will find extraordinary power and strength that can withstand any form of opposition to your life's progress. Make it your duty to build your character. Your character will either attract people to you or repel them. The people matrix is a person's ability to harness power and strength through the relationships they build, by which they can create spiritual leverage for themselves and break the chains of defeat and failure.

Let's revisit another principle we previously discussed that will help shape your character and give you the strength of inner character. Our generation seldom talk about character because of the demands required to build it. We are used to shortcuts and fast food, wanting to translate everything into something FAST. However, life is built on character, and spiritual strength has its origin in a person's faith. Faith is the ultimate requirement for anyone who has decided to live above mediocrity and attract a life of victory and testimonies.

Your ability to handle tests and trials through faith is a remarkable trait that must be fulfilled before you can experience a life of unlimited possibilities and opportunities. I am here to show you how your faith fits into the matrix of your battle against the cycle of defeat. How does faith fit in, and how can it fit in properly? Hebrews 11.6 says, "But without faith it is impossible to please Him, for he who comes to God must believe that He is, and that He is a rewarder of those who diligently seek Him." There is only one thing that pleases and honours God more than anything else: your faith.

Faith is of a man's heart. It is not logic or sense; faith is absolute trust in the ability and capability of God. Faith tells us that God exists and that He is a reality, but it also assures us that God's power and ability to transform your life is certain and undeniable. There are three keys that make your faith true. Do you know them? If you did, what would you do? What investment are you willing to make in these important things? There is a cost to everything important. Are you willing to pay that price? Many people fail in life because they are not willing to pay the ultimate price. Success and victory are costly. It is expensive and taxing to want to be successful. It is not a walk in the park, nor is it dessert, which is the last of lasts and you can either go with or without it. The cost of success is not like that. It is the price required before one can embark on the journey of life.

I am here to challenge you to develop the mindset and character necessary for your victory over the cycle of defeat. What faith is needed to give your character the force of power required to leverage

THE SECRET OF BREAKING THE CYCLE OF DEFEAT | 77

your life to a higher dimension of productivity and success? I speak of the "Trinity of Faith." True faith is bound by three key principles: the union of the heart, the mind, and the mouth. This is clearly set out in the book of Deuteronomy 30:11–14: "For this commandment which I command you today is not too mysterious for you, nor is it far off. It is not in heaven, that you should say, 'Who will ascend into heaven for us and bring it to us, that we may hear it and do it?' Nor is it beyond the sea, that you should say, 'Who will go over the sea for us and bring it to us, that we may hear it and do it?' But the word is very near you, in your mouth and in your heart, that you may do it." Faith is conceived in a man's heart, refined in his mind, and released through his mouth or lips. These three must agree—your heart, your mind, and your mouth.

Therefore, guard your heart, for "out of it spring the issues of life" (Prov. 4.23). Whatever a man thinketh in his heart, so is he (Prov.23.7). The heart is the combustion chamber of life, the mind is the fire or the wood that burns in the chamber, and the mouth is the release valve, enabling the chamber to release what is made inside of it. Such is the Trinity of Faith. When faith is properly incubated in one's life, it gives birth to an Intense desire to build character. Without true faith, no one, absolutely no one, can have the desire or courage to build character. Once character is formed and built, the sky is the limit.

Invest endless effort into building your character and attitude; in the end, this will pay off. The great heroes of faith were men and women of great character. They deliberately and intentionally invested in their character, and the outcome of their lives has mesmerized many people throughout generations. The focus of Elisha in following Elijah is a testimony, as is the courage of Esther in the face of death, the commitment of Ruth in the midst of despair and hopelessness, the integrity of Joseph in the midst of extreme provocation and temptation, and the faith of Abraham in the face of seeming delay and frustration. When you strive to build character and attitude, you open your life to horizons of endless possibilities.

Do not waste your time, and do not take shortcuts, allowing Satan to deceive you. Do not bow to the credit card mentality of "enjoy now and pay later," as this will ultimately prove costly and dangerous. Here is my advice to sum it up: Do all you can to build your character. Character is like savings—you will always find it handy on a rainy day. Your character is a master key that can open endless doors of human endeavour. Keep it on your side and keep it intact. You will need it. Grow it, nurture it, and live by it. In the end, character is everything.

8

The Hidden Mystery of Thanksgiving

"Life is like riding a bicycle. to keep balance you must keep moving" Albert Einstein

Life is like a kernel of wheat. Many concern themselves with what is on the outside, but the wise will break the kernel to discover what is inside. The real value of the kernel is not what is on the outside; it is what is on the inside. Today, the church is full of superficial Christianity. To involve oneself in superficiality is to involve oneself in triviality. The outside may look good, but the inside is often rotten to the core. Our Christianity lacks depth—real spiritual depth. This is because our generation is unwilling to do what it takes to have depth of spiritual understanding, character, and insight. Many are not willing to pay the price to acquire the inner spiritual strength that will move their lives beyond the basic, elementary aspects of human existence toward a life of depth and spiritual insights.

It takes time and discipline to search for something meaningful. It takes time and effort to break the kernel of wheat and enjoy what is inside. Life must have a purpose and meaning far beyond the usual day-to-day happenings. As Scripture says, "Deep calls unto deep" (Ps. 42.7). Is there depth in your life? Is there depth and purpose in your life? Is there clarity and direction in your purpose? To get answers, we must ask questions and these must be real questions. But how do you get to that place where you can unravel your life's purpose, meaning, and direction? There is a price you must pay in order for you to reach that level. There is a level of strict training and discipline that is required to get you there. You have to spend countless hours preparing and planning your next move. You must develop the skill of crafting your life and packaging it in a way that will attract the greatness and success God has intended for you.

As you seek to figure things out, it is important not to lose sight of God. Without God, you can be rest assured that life is damned. So, what then, can you do to avoid the syndrome of defeat and frustration? Many in this generation have given up on life and on hope. They are merely living, unsure of what tomorrow holds or whether tomorrow holds anything for them at all. This is the state many people find themselves in—life is just there, but it lacks real meaning and direction. Many have unknowingly resigned themselves to fate.

But I am glad you reading this book. The mere fact that you are reading this book is a clear sign that God has a purpose for you. God wants you to defeat the cycle of defeat and failure and unleash the full potential of your life. But are you willing to pay the price? Are you willing to go through the process? Daniel was willing to go through the fiery furnace to become what God had called him to be. Because he was willing to go through the tests and trials, he was unwilling to break spiritual protocol or law, or take shortcuts. Whatever it took, Daniel was willing to pay the price. What price are you paying to achieve greatness? What effort have you made to release your life from the cage of defeat?

You have to make up your mind. You cannot do anything significant if your mind is not made up. You cannot go far with an undecided mind. If you do not make up your mind, the devil will make it up for you. Many people have allowed the devil to make up their mind for them because they kept procrastinating, never making up their mind, and Satan took advantage of their valley of indecision. Satan likes to exploit uncertainties and confusion; he is the master of it and a deceptor of not. To defeat Satan and his schemes, one must necessarily and without the avoidance of doubt, make up their mind. Success is 90 percent of making up one's mind and 10 percent of human effort. No human effort will make meaning unless one's mind is made up. You too need to make up your mind to live a life of gratitude and thanksgiving.

The hidden mystery of thanksgiving has not been adequately understood by many in the Christian faith today. The subject of Thanksgiving is not one that Christians want to talk about. Many Christians prefer to talk about their problems—how much of problems they have, how things have gone wrong, how life is unfair, how much pain they are in, and how they seem to be on the receiving end of life. As a result, they unconsciously acquire a victim mentality, enlisting sympathy rather than empathy. At this level of thinking, life seems hopeless and meaningless.

Do you feel defeated and frustrated? Are you tempted to give up? What can you do to get your life back on track and break the cycle of defeat? It starts with you understanding the power of thanksgiving. The power of Thanksgiving is realized when you know that everything big always starts small. Every journey of faith begins with one step of faith. It also involves the ability to recognize the power of small things. If you cannot see the power of small things and of humble beginnings, you cannot achieve greatness. Scripture says, "For who has despised the day of small things?" (Zech. 4.10). Everything big always starts small. Begin each day with a heart full of gratitude and thanksgiving. Although this may seem small and common, the mystery behind it is often overlooked and misunderstood.

As you continue reading this part of the book, I urge you to pause and reflect. This is not a casual reflection I am talking about, but a deep, serious, and soul-searching endeavour. Ask yourself, "Where am I in relation to the subject at hand? How well have I acquitted myself?" In this context, you must ask yourself difficult and personal questions, holding yourself accountable for your actions. Many Christians prefer to live their lives without accountability. Yet what pleases you does not necessarily please everyone, and what pleases you does not often please God. Accountability is the antidote to the chaos and confusion we often experience in our lives.

Thanksgiving is an often forgotten virtue. How often, when we are in trouble, do we remember those who helped us before? In most cases, once we are out of trouble, we often change our posture and scarcely remember what our situation was like. The psalmist said, "What shall I render to the Lord for all His benefits toward me?" (Ps. 116.12). This was the reflection of someone who realized that someone—God—was responsible and was the source behind their victory, and they needed to acknowledge it. From Genesis to Revelation, we see God at work, redeeming and releasing people. Yet over and over again, humanity has a convenient error of forgetting and falling back into the same old struggles.

The Israelites suffered under the weight of Pharaoh's abusive system of slavery and cried out to the Lord. Their taskmasters increased their work, extracting labour from them at a costly price. In Exodus 3:9, we read, "Now therefore, behold, the cry of the children of Israel has come to Me, and I have also seen the oppression with which the Egyptians oppress them." God heard their cry and sent Moses to deliver them from Pharaoh. After ten severe plagues, Pharaoh finally let the Israelites go. God, in His love for His people, set them free.

Yet as soon as the people were free and descended into the wilderness, they forgot what God had done for them and began murmuring. Because of His love for them, God took them through the wilderness. Though it seemed long-winded, He was showing them mercy and favour. In Exodus 13.17–18, we read, "Then it came to pass, when Pharaoh had let the people go, that God did not lead them by way of the land of the Philistines, although that was near; for God said, 'Lest perhaps the people change their minds when they see war, and return to Egypt.' So God led the people around by way of the wilderness of the Red Sea."

Despite God's merciful guidance, the people still forgot His goodness. In Exodus 14.11-12, they cried out, "Because there were no graves in Egypt, have you taken us away to die in the wilderness? Why have you so dealt with us, to bring us up out of Egypt? Is this not the word that we told you in Egypt, saying, 'Let us alone that we may serve the Egyptians'? For it would have been better for us to serve the Egyptians than that we should die in the wilderness." Their forgetfulness and murmuring continued throughout their journey to the Promised Land. In Numbers 11.1-6, we read, "Now when the people complained, it displeased the Lord... And the children of Israel also wept again and said: 'Who will give us meat to eat? We remember the fish which we ate freely in Egypt... but now our whole being is dried up; there is nothing at all except this manna before our eyes!'" The pattern of forgetfulness, murmuring and ingratitude that seemed to have animated the people of Israel, seemed like a curse that would not go away.

The Bible is filled with stories of God's spectacular deliverance and the stark contrast of man's ungratefulness. I have often experienced the bitter poison of ingratitude firsthand. You would think people would learn from the mistakes of yesterday, but alas, we seem to glide easily into the path of ingratitude. This reflects our inner struggle with pride and arrogance. Left to his own devices, man is a gathering danger to himself. The chalice of ingratitude has poisoned and ruined the lives of many Christians. It seems to me that this is Satan's most charming weapon for holding Christians back in a conundrum or vicious cycle of defeat. When we forget our yesterday's benefactors and pain bearers, we ruin the possibilities of a better future.

The struggle between God and Israel can also be seen as a struggle between a living God and the arrogance and pride of an ungrateful nation. The danger of forgetting what God did yesterday is a looming danger in every Christian's life. So, how do we cure this cancer? How do we cure the cancerous tumour that threatens to ruin human life?

Now let me discuss the gimel of Thanksgiving and give full meaning to our discussion. Remember the power of number three as we discussed in the previous chapter. Let's examine and illuminate the concept and the key called thanksgiving. What place does it hold in the battle against the vicious cycle of defeat? How can one use it as leverage and a weapon to fight the demonic forces of darkness, stagnation and failure? How can one also release its full potential and power to help fight the vicious cycle of defeat? Thanksgiving is made up of three key virtues: remembrance, gratitude, and praise (or adoration). With this understanding, we can easily come up with a mathematical concept for defining and understanding what is thanksgiving and why should it be an important aspect or key in fighting the cycle of defeat:

Remembrance + gratitude + praise (Adoration) = Thanksgiving

Let me take a moment to define these three key concepts and locate them in the battle against the cycle of defeat and failure for you.

Remembrance is the art of recollection and reminiscence of past events—When we look back to see what happened in times past. Our memories keep alive the wonderful things God and our fellow human beings have done in our lives. Many nations observe Remembrance Day to commemorate something wonderful, epic or significant that happened in the past. In a similar way, God instructed the children of Israel to build a memorial lest they would forget how God had fought for them. When we forget, we no doubt glide into the valley of ingratitude and murmuring. Oftentimes, our lives are hindered because we often forget the people who stood with us at the most difficult part of our life and destroy our foundation, unconsciously. Avoid this trap of the enemy.

Gratitude is the art of appreciation. It is an expression of thanksgiving or thankfulness. While **praise** or **adoration** is an act of elevating the one to whom we are grateful. You are in awe of their action towards you and you cannot afford but to lift them up to the highest place of honour, which will result in deep thanksgiving.

Now, let me take you through a personal experience to show you how important Thanksgiving is to fighting the cycle of defeat and failure. My personal history—my autobiography—is animated with remarkable stories of the sacrifices many people have made in my life. Men and women who helped and lifted me in the darkest hours of my life. I often acknowledge them as part of my life's story, and, where possible, I remind them and myself of what they have done for me. This is the secret I have learned that has revolutionized and changed my life and the prospects of my future. Consider the story of Joseph Finichio, who helped me purchase 429 Barton Street East, a large warehouse, when I had only known him for less than two months. He listened to my story with compassion and understanding and pushed me to the next level of my spiritual journey. How can I forget such people or take their generosity for granted? The opposite is very true in the lives of many Christians and we also read such stories in the Bible with consternation and shock.

Consider Jesus' interaction with the ten lepers—men who had suffered indignation, shame and humiliation in the community they lived. They were often isolated and degraded. By one simple request, Jesus changed their lives by healing all of them, but only one returned—to the shock of our master Jesus Christ. How could they so easily forget such gesture of kindness? How could they neglect such kind of love and generosity? This seems to be the tragedy of human life. After healing them and seeing their attitude, Jesus was forced to ask a simple question, "Were there not ten cleansed? But where are the nine?" (Luke 17.17). Our ingratitude has often closed doors for us and sometimes we have found ourselves struggling and cannot go back to the people who helped us yesterday, because of our ungratefulness. In this story of the ten lepers, only one returned to give thanks. The other nine quickly forgot their hour of leprosy and acted with pride and arrogance. Let's be honest: do you struggle with this kind of behaviour or attitude? It seems to me that life is full of such examples. Jesus also rebuked the cities of Chorazin and Bethsaida, saying, "Woe to you, Chorazin! Woe to you, Bethsaida! For if the mighty works which were done in you had been done in Tyre and Sidon, they would have repented long ago" (Matt. 11.21). Ingratitude can also occur when we take for granted the kindness and mercy God has shown us in times past. This was the case in the city of Chorazin and Bethsaida. Familiarity breeds contempt; but the more we are thankful, the closer we are to God and the more strength and power we have in fighting the cycle of defeat and failure.

Ingratitude has cost us opportunities and the possibility of lifting up our lives. I have seen this mistake countless times—people focus endlessly on the sideshows of life, neglecting the vital virtue of thanksgiving. But thanksgiving is a key, a real master key that unlocks doors and opportunities. Most people who have made it to the top are people who are thankful.

Consider Esther, who was grateful and thankful to her uncle Mordecai and was unwilling to let him down in the hour of need. She risked her life to show gratitude. Ruth followed Naomi and showed gratitude to her mother-in-law by committing herself to her cause. Her gratitude eventually paid off and she became the wife of Boaz, and by that association, the great-grandmother of our Lord Jesus Christ. David was grateful to the kindness of Jonathan, that years after the death of Jonathan, he sought out and cared for Jonathan's descendants. He was not willing to neglect an act of kindness that had secured his life.

Yet, how often do we forget and trivialize the heroes of yesterday, and in so doing, burn our bridges for tomorrow? The Roman philosopher Cicero once said, "Gratitude is not only the greatest of virtues but the parent of all others." How, then, can we be grateful? How do we develop it? As with any skill, practice makes perfect. Norman Vincent Peale wisely noted, "The more you practice the art of thanksgiving, the more you have to be thankful for." An anonymous writer remarked, "Gratitude makes what we have enough." It is clear, that the more we practice gratitude, the more ammunition we have against the cycle of defeat. The cycle of defeat cannot stand before a heart that is full of gratitude.

One of the greatest mistakes we can make in life is to trivialize the sacrifice of others for our own comfort. This is the capriciousness of the human soul. Ungratefulness is indeed a negative emotion that every human being must avoid and fight. Let the floodgates of heaven open by you blowing the trumpet of gratitude in your heart. A grateful person never loses friends, neither will they lose battles—they always find a helping hand in every situation. The only way you can fight failure successfully is to keep gratitude at the forefront of your life's battles. Never be tempted to forget yesterday's good because of today's mistakes. Never be tempted to forget yesterday's kindness because of today's misunderstandings.

I have seen humanity's propensity for error when it comes to handling gratitude. Gratitude withheld is gratitude ruined, and gratitude ruined is always followed by a ruined destiny. Change your philosophy; let gratitude be the breastplate of your heart and thankfulness the crown you wear—not to elevate yourself, but to lift and honour those who stood by you in the hour of need. Gratitude has a tendency to turn even your deadliest enemies into your closest friends. A man who is grateful lacks nothing in his life because life itself pours out favour upon him.

Ingratitude often ruins even the greatest heroes. Many find themselves stuck between a rock and a hard place because they fail to acknowledge past kindness. Gratitude must never grow tired, It must never become old and grey-haired. Gratitude is meant to be always present and alive. The cycle of defeat melts in the face of a heart full of thankfulness, and gratitude. Sometimes, we have to be grateful for things we do not have, for in our lack we may learn the value of stewardship and the importance of what we need. As Paul says, "In everything give thanks; for this is the will of God in Christ Jesus for you" (1 Thess. 5.18).

Gratitude shows maturity and wisdom. The more mature we are, the greater our gratitude.

9

The People Matrix

The Unknown Secret of the Power of People

"People count and matter in everyone's story. The outcome of your destiny is ultimately shaped by God and people. Watch your relationships, for they will either make or unmake you. People can either ruin you or lift you to unimaginable heights." —Prof. Tom Tirivangani.

The path to success in human life is filled with many pitfalls and challenges. It often presents you with detours and sometimes roadblocks. As Mandela once remarked, "There is no easy walk to freedom." I would add, "There is no easy walk to success and to breaking the cycle of defeat." Success calls for ingenuity in your thinking and your approach. It calls for and demands an uncommon approach to life and to the situations that often confront us. Your ability and wisdom in dealing with the challenges you face in your fight against the cycle of defeat and failure will ultimately determine the outlook of your life. As someone once said, "Life is what you make of it." There is no strict formula for success, but there are principles and secrets, and how you apply these principles depends on the person dealing with these storms and challenges of life.

In the process of fighting for a better future and a better life, we must learn and unlearn many things in the process. It is important, however, to keep your mind focused. The goal is to defeat the cycle of defeat and failure and live a life of victory and success. The Word of God says, "Looking unto Jesus, the author and finisher of our faith" (Heb. 12.2). When you lose sight of the goal, you have already lost the battle. Focus determines the outcome. Focus is an antidote to failure and ruin. When you lose sight of God, you have already capitulated to the grand scheme of the devil. When Satan seduces and convinces you to take your eyes off Christ and instead fixate on your problems, your weaknesses, your pain, and your struggles, he has taken hold of you by the collar, and it will be difficult to escape from his grip.

When Satan convinces you that "so and so" is evil and that you need to avoid them, he has drawn you into his trap. If Satan manages to convince you that all your suffering is caused by people, he has already poisoned your mind. When he succeeds in shifting your focus from himself and the spiritual warfare to the perceived weaknesses of a brother or sister, he has spoiled your chances of breaking the cycle of defeat.

I urge you to read this book carefully and with intentionality. The words here are both spirit and life, containing secrets that are revolutionary and life-changing. They may appear simple, yet their impact is profound. Remember, dynamite often comes in small packages, and if you don't read with spiritual alertness and attentiveness, you will miss the nuggets enunciated here that are likely to change your life forever.

Stop everything you're doing and find a quiet place to read this book, and do not take this lightly. You must actually do it! Now that you've reached chapter 8, consider this a checkpoint. How have you been reading this book? I suspect that because of the way you've been reading this book, you may have missed a lot of important things. But it is not too late, reset your mind, change your approach, and recover the things you may have overlooked. The information contained here is a pure gem, a diamond of rare quality and value. Mindset is a rare and often misunderstood virtue and concept. I will guide you in this part of the book on how you can reset your mind, read this book with purpose, and see the real value of your time and effort. Expect the unexpected, for this part of the book, is meant to bring things together, giving you leverage that will change you forever.

If you knew you were about to discover a rare secret or principle that would change your life, what would you do? Understand this principle: nothing is important until you make it important. When you allow familiarity to take over your human analysis and effort, you risk losing opportunities and missing life's potential. Nothing in life becomes meaningful until you assign it meaning. Great people are not great in everyone's eyes; they are great to those who recognize their true value.

A diamond is just a piece of stone to someone who does not know its real and intrinsic value. To someone, rare gold may just be a piece of ordinary stone, that is why it is said, "Another men's trash would be another man's treasure. Therefore, it pays to know the value of things, and it pays even more to recognize the true value of people in your life. I remember when I graduated from law school, and ranked at the top of my class and was the best law graduate in the country that year. I entered the marketplace full of idealism, only to learn the vast difference between idealism and reality, between perception and fact just a few months into my career. Now that I am older and more mature, I prefer reality to idealism. People matter— whether we acknowledge it positively or negatively, this truth is unavoidable.

I reached the top of my legal career and became an instant hit in the legal profession due to the guidance of one man: Mr. Rushwaya Rushwaya, an old but experienced legal clerk with twenty-five years of service when I met him. To someone else, he might have been just an old legal clerk; to me, he was a mentor who taught me how to interview clients, how to give legal advice, how to draft court pleadings, and ultimately how to present cases before judges. I must say I learnt quite a great deal from him. Many people miss their path because they do not understand the "people matrix" and they do not understand the true value of people. Remember, no man is an island; no one has ever achieved success without people. Paradoxically, many have also failed because of the people.

Consider David, who became king because of the kindness and love of Jonathan. Jonathan risked his life and defied his father, King Saul, to protect David. Additionally, the men of war who followed David, men who were at his side, men who were determined to see him succeed and become King. As recorded in 1 Chronicles 12.38–40, "All these men of war who could keep ranks came to Hebron with a loyal heart, to make David king over all Israel; and all the rest of Israel were of one mind to make David king. And they were there with David three days, eating and drinking, for their brethren had prepared for them." Without the sacrifice and determination of these men, David's dream would have been a nightmare.

Apostle Paul, too, was saved by people who risked their life to save his life—his nephew exposed a plot by more than forty men who had sworn to neither eat nor drink until they had killed Paul (Acts 23.12-16). Life is indeed mysterious; people we often overlook and see no value in them, may be the very heroes and benefactors God has placed in our path to lift us up to another level. Consider the story of Saul. Saul's life also was changed the day he met Samuel the prophet. What began as a simple search for your lost donkeys became a crowning of kingship. Saul set out as an ordinary man and returned a crowned and anointed King. Similarly, you may be searching for "lost donkeys," but God has a surprise for you.

People are often the miracles in our life's journey. We cannot reach the pinnacle of our human achievement without knowing and recognizing the value of people in the struggle against the cycle of defeat. Consider Rahab, a mere prostitute whose kindness and generosity to the Israelite spies altered her destiny and life (Jos 2.1-14). Similarly, in the course of ministering to her mother-in-law, Naomi, Ruth met her destiny and became what she never imagined she could be. She married Boaz and became the great-grandmother of Jesus Christ. People are the bridge we desperately need to use to reach the other side of human existence. Your ability to relate with people, to see their real value, and to learn from their skills, compassion, and generosity will determine how high you can climb the ladder of human achievement or how far you can go in your life.

Paul advised the Philippian Church with these words: "Let this mind be in you which was also in Christ Jesus" (Phil. 2.5). Our human relationships are keys that God uses to release our life to the next level. God always puts people in our paths, and there is nothing, absolutely nothing meaningful we can achieve in life without people. The Shunamite woman ministered to Elisha, and her hospitality to an anointed man of God changed her life forever. God used Elisha to transform her from barrenness to fruitfulness, from shame to honour (2 Kings 4.8-17). How are you treating people you meet on the way? Do you think you have a positive or negative "people matrix"? Watch this carefully because ultimately, people will determine the outcome of your destiny.

People have the power to lift you up or to ruin you. The destiny of Joseph was almost ruined by the jealousy of his brothers and the lust of Potiphar's wife. Samson was brought down by a prostitute called Delilah, a woman he trusted yet one who sought his downfall. King Ahab's destiny was ruined by his wife Jezebel, while Jesus was ultimately betrayed by one of his closest associates and disciples, Judas Iscariot. Yet, Jesus' ministry was enlarged and expanded by twelve ordinary men who understood His vision and passion, and made the necessary sacrifice. Similarly, the Bible was written by forty men who carried divine truths in their hearts and would not settle for less. A period of 1500 years and three separate continents —Africa, Europe and Asia, could not deter God's vision for humanity. In this we see the humanity of God, that instead of putting pen and paper himself, he chose 40 frail men to write his story. Indeed, "we have this treasure in earthen vessels" (2 Cor. 4.7). As you fight the cycle of defeat, you need to recognize that you cannot do it alone. Arrogance, the crown of fools, would make one believe they need no one. No matter how powerful and anointed you are, people matter—the good and the bad alike. In life, sometimes things happen between us and other people that we cannot control, but God has given us the power and ability to choose how we respond to them. I often say that our life depends on two relationships: the vertical relationship, meaning our relationship with God, and the horizontal relationship, our relationship with others. The cross is the meeting place between our vertical and our horizontal relationships, and at their meeting point, life is made and its meaning extracted.

To illustrate this, let's draw the cross to underscore the significance of this idea. The Gospel begins and ends with the cross of Jesus Christ, one of the most significant events in human history.

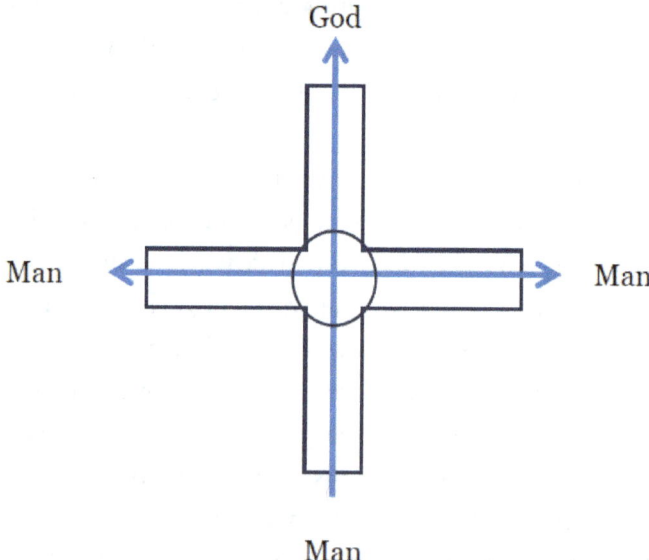

In the cross of Christ, we find purpose, meaning, and the power and anointing to break the cycle of defeat. The more we meditate on the cross, our relationship with God, and our relationship with our fellow men, the more power that is released to us and the more ammunition and strength we have in fighting the cycle of defeat and failure. Our relationship with God is the foundation of our victory, and our relationship with others is the key that unlocks what God has promised for us. Stop locking yourself in the prison of bitterness and anger, the conflict and strife, in order for you to fight effectively the battle for your destiny.

Just remember this: in your journey of life and in your battle against the cycle of defeat and failure, you are going to meet good and bad people. It's not what they do to you that matters, but it's how you respond to them that really matters. Your response is the crown you will wear—it can be one of gold or diamond, or it can be a crown of straw or plastic, the choice is yours. Your perspective, your response and how you view things are a real danger, and can either make you bitter or better.

The powerful and amazing classical advice of Paul the Apostle is worth noting here. He had provided this powerful teaching after having spent many years of his ministry undertaking missionary journeys. He often depended on people on his journeys and the success of his journeys depended on people—strangers who became friends, and benefactors and acquaintances who became like family. Yet, Paul also faced some of his greatest persecutions from people. Reflecting on his experiences, he recounts the suffering he endured in Philippi, where he and his companions were "outrageously treated." He writes, "For you yourselves know, brethren, that our coming to you was not in vain. But even after we had suffered before and were spitefully treated at Philippi, as you know, we were bold in our God to speak to you the gospel of God in much conflict. For our exhortation did not come from error or uncleanness, nor was it in deceit" (1 Thess. 2.1-3).

In contrast, the Galatian church treated Paul with love and compassion. He wrote in Galatians 4.13-14, describing how they welcomed him "as an angel of God": "You know that because of physical infirmity I preached the gospel to you at the first. And my trial which was in my flesh you did not despise or reject, but you received me as an angel of God, even as Christ Jesus."

Towards the end of his life, filled with experience, wisdom, and understanding of the value of people in our journey, Paul wrote powerfully in his renowned Letter to the Romans. This letter is pregnant with insight and revelation, which are essential for life to be meaningful. Revelations and wisdom are like spices to your food; without them, our food will be tasteless and a pain to those who participate in the table of our human life. In Romans 12: 9-21. Paul writes:

> "Let love be without hypocrisy. Abhor what is evil. Cling to what is good. Be kindly affectionate to one another with brotherly love, in honor giving preference to one another; not lagging in diligence, fervent in spirit, serving the Lord; rejoicing in hope, patient in tribulation, continuing steadfastly in prayer; distributing to the needs of the saints, given to hospitality. "Bless those who persecute you; bless and do not curse. Rejoice with those who rejoice, and weep with those who weep. Be of the same mind toward one another. Do not set your mind on high things, but associate with the humble. Do not be wise in your own opinion. "Repay no one evil for evil. Have regard for good things in the sight of all men. If it is possible, as much as depends on you, live peaceably with all men. Beloved, do not avenge yourselves, but rather give place to wrath; for it is written, 'Vengeance is Mine, I will repay,' says the Lord. Therefore 'If your enemy is hungry, feed him; If he is thirsty, give him a drink; For in so doing you will heap coals of fire on his head.' "Do not be overcome by evil, but overcome evil with good."

There are many secrets we can extrapolicate from this sacred scripture. Let's identify them:

1. Love must be sincere and not hypocritical. It is easy to pretend to love than to love sincerely.

2. Real love must lead to devotion to one another. When love for one another doesn't result in deepening our commitment to one another, our love is just mere human love.

3. We are to bless those who persecute us and strive at all costs to live in harmony with others. This can only be possible if one practices humility and not revenge.

4. Do what is right in the eyes of everyone. Our integrity and sincerity will win us friends and benefactors.

When reading Romans 12, I feel like I am reading the corpus of wisdom on how we can develop our human relationships that will help us gain leverage in the fight against the cycle of defeat. Many Christians are frustrated and are experiencing the endless and vicious Cycle of defeat; because they mishandle people and often disregard those who should matter to them. I have personally been persecuted and vilified by those I have made huge sacrifices for. I have been betrayed by people that I have risked my personal life trying to rescue. The vilest of comments and remarks I have received came from those I sincerely love the most, the ones I thought knew me and understood my motive.

It is interesting to read of King David's experiences. He sheds light to the struggles at the core of human life in Psalms 35.11-16:

"Fierce witnesses rise up; they ask me things that I do not know. They reward me evil for good, to the sorrow of my soul. But as for me, when they were sick, my clothing was sackcloth; I humbled myself with fasting; and my prayer would return to my own heart. I paced about as though he were my friend or brother; I bowed down heavily, as one who mourns for his mother. But in my adversity they rejoiced and gathered together; attackers gathered against me, and I did not know it; they tore at me and did not cease; with ungodly mockers at feasts. They gnashed at me with their teeth."

We see the pain and anguish David felt, the terrible experiences he endured at the hands of others. Yet, despite this, he still asks, "Is there still anyone who is left of the house of Saul, that I may show him kindness for Jonathan's sake?" (2 Sam. 9.1). David's example urges us not to be quick to condemn or dismiss others, for God's blessing is often hidden in people—sometimes in the most unlikely individuals and families. Who could have imagined that in Saul's family, someone could love David as Jonathan did? Life is full of surprises; therefore, walk with care and wisdom.

I would like to conclude with a few words of wisdom from Yu Tzu, "Every day I examine myself on three counts. In what I have undertaken on another's behalf, have I failed to do my best? In my dealings with my friends have I failed to be trustworthy in what I say? Have I passed on to others anything that I have not tried out myself? The Master said: 'In ruling a state of a thousand chariots, approach your duties with reverence and be trustworthy in what you say; avoid excesses in expenditures and love your fellow men; employ the labour of the common people only in the right seasons.'" I therefore urge you to refine your relationship with people.

10

Prophecy as Both Knife and Medicine

"By a prophet, the Lord brought Israel out of Egypt, and by a prophet he was preserved" (Hos. 12.13)

Have you ever wondered and said to yourself, "My lot is too much? My burden too big to bear?" Have you ever been driven to despair by life's challenges and storms? Are you feeling overwhelmed and unsure about your next step in life? Are you asking, "God, where are You? Don't You care that we perish?"

This part of the book is inspired by the Holy Spirit, specifically prepared and written for people like you. You may feel as though life has thrown you into the valley of dry bones, like the prophet Ezekiel, or you may be thinking, like Elijah or Jonah, "God, let me die." I want to assure you that at the times when God seems silent and distant, God is, in fact, ever so present and close to you. When it feels as though God does not care, as you navigate the turbulent and stormy seas of life, He is whispering to you in the inner ear of your spirit.

God is spirit, and it is His habit to speak to your spirit, not to your flesh. Many people often miss God because they pretend to be spiritual, yet they are carnal and fleshly. They speak faith, yet their hearts swell with doubt and unbelief; they confess love, yet their hearts swell with bitterness and hatred. They have not learned to love without hypocrisy. If you are such a person who speaks what is not in your heart, you will never be able to engage God. God minds more what is in your heart than what is in on your lips. If you want to know God, God prefers to be known through your heart. It's the heart that counts to Him.

I have often said that to know God is to know the way out. To know Jesus Christ is to see the way out. Thomas, one of Jesus Christ's eminent disciples— an inquisitive restless man, always desiring to have the depths of spiritual understanding— asked his Master, "How can we know the way? How can we know where You are going?" This probing question, well thought out and a carefully articulated question brought forth Jesus's epic response, which I call the "response of responses, a master of all": "I am the way, the truth, and the life" (John 14.6). How can you see the way out of the valley of dry bones unless you know the Way, so that you can see your way out of the cycle of defeat?

Remember what I said in Chapter 7 about the power of three in Hebrew. The number three, gimel in Hebrew, signifies divine completeness or perfection. Here lie three great ideas and mysteries of life that Jesus Christ identifies Himself with: He is "the way, the truth, and the life" (John 14.6). In knowing Jesus Christ as our Master and Savior, we come to know the truth. When we have the truth in our hearts, we begin to see the way out of confusion and darkness. Beyond the confusion and darkness, we enter into a realm of life —a real, meaningful life worth living. We cease to merely exist in the world and become a meaningful part of God's epic and grand design that we call life.

God is concerned about you, no matter how often or how many times the devil has deceived you into believing that God does not care. The enemy may tell you that God is unfair, and somehow, He has forsaken you and your family, and that it's better to put matters into your own hands because this God is distant and uncaring. Sadly, the majority of born-again believers are people who have put matters in their own hands. They are driven by self. I mean, self-deception is more dangerous than just deception. A person who is self-deluded has no way of knowing that they are deluded, except by the grace of God, who allows them to see what they cannot see, perhaps to understand what they cannot understand.

I always warn people: be careful not to enter into self-deception. When you fall into that trap, it is difficult to come out. This is what happened when the Israelites fell into the deception of idolatry and Baalism. They thought they were praying, but it was mere ritualism. Scripture illustrates this well in the story of Elijah and the prophets of Baal. Elijah mocked and teased their gods, saying, "Cry aloud, for he is a god; either he is meditating, or he is busy, or he is on a journey, or perhaps he is sleeping and must be awakened" (1 Kings 18.27). But the God of Israel is different. He is not a god but he is God. He is living, alive and active and powerful.

God is the Word that became flesh, and He does nothing without His Word. He is the God who cared about the bareness of the Shunammite woman, sending Elisha to her and her family. He is the God who promotes, and He sent Samuel the prophet to anoint Saul. He is God who heals, and he sent Elisha to heal Naaman of leprosy. He sent His Son to heal the ten lepers, to restore the eyes of Bartimaeus, son of Timaeus. He had compassion on Mary Magdalene, the prostitute who became the minister.

God cares for you beyond human imagination and comprehension. He sent His Son, Jesus Christ, to die for your sins—to become the sacrifice that breaks the yoke of guilt and death. How could such a God not care about you? Paul writes movingly in Romans 8.32: "He who did not spare His own Son, but delivered Him up for us all, how shall He not with Him also freely give us all things?" It is clear that God cares, and His care surpasses all understanding. Yet, the devil—your arch-enemy, the betrayer and deceiver—tries to make you doubt God's sincerity and love. Satan manipulates and twists things to portray this awesome God in bad light.

I have encountered people who are possessed by Lucifer and anointed by the devil himself, accuse the innocent and portray them as guilty as sin itself. You wonder, "What has become of humanity?" David himself cried out in anguish in Psalms 35. 11-12, "Fierce witnesses rise up; they ask me things that I do not know. They reward me evil for good." I, too, have tasted this bitter gall of life, driven to despair, questioning through the night, "What's wrong with humanity? Why do those who proclaim Christ seem to be working even harder for the devil?" This is the paradox of life and you need to unravel this mystery and see beyond human appearances, if you are to break the cycle of defeat.

You cannot be a superficial Christian; there is no room for shallowness in the Kingdom of God. Satan wants to hold you onto appearances, stirring up storms in your life and then questioning you, "Do you see? God doesn't care. If He did, why are you going through what you are going through?" You quickly forget that it was Satan who threw you into trouble to begin with. Remember that, though, he inflicted Job with sickness and disease, it was also him who then used the people Job loved so much to say, "Curse God and die" (Job 2.9). This is why our Christianity must go beyond the surface. As Paul says, "Leaving the discussion of the elementary principles of Christ, let us go on to perfection, not laying again the foundation of repentance from dead works and of faith toward God" (Heb. 6.1).

Have you moved beyond the elementary principles of life? Have you become mature? Can you see beyond your situation and understand that, even though Job suffered disaster, God still cared so much about him?

You may ask, "If God cares, why didn't He stop the devil from destroying Job's family? Why did Job suffer all that loss?" I will hasten to tell you that character, strength, and integrity are often forged through life's experiences. Here is the true value of experience, "Experience is not what happens to a man, it's what a man does with what happens to him." God knows best what is best for us, even when we cannot see the full picture. He wants us to trust Him and believe Him, that in the midst of the storm of life, He is with us. He is true to His word that He will not leave us or forsake us, and that He is with us till the end of time. Jesus says, "Count it all joy when you fall into various trials, knowing that the testing of your faith produces patience" (Jas. 1.2).

Now comes the important part we have been waiting for. The title of our message is that prophesy is both a knife and medicine. How is this possible and what is the meaning of all this? No prophet ever came for the sake of just coming. Every time God sends a prophet, it is a mark of His genuine desire to deliver His people out of bondage, and out of the cycle of defeat and failure. David acknowledges in Psalms 34.19: "Many are the afflictions of the righteous, but the Lord delivers him out of them all." You may still ask, "Why does God allow afflictions and then deliver us? Does he just want to prove himself? Well enough, I do not want a God who allows me to suffer and then come to help me. Why can't he just stop the suffering period? Understand that man's character and deeds are a snare to him. There is no one who can bear the consequences of sin unless sin is found even in his bloodline. Man is the author of his own misfortune. Yet, out of His unfailing love, God always rescues us, even when we do not deserve it.

John Wesley wrote, "The mind does not see either the beauties or the terrors of eternity, because they are so distant from us. It is as if they had no existence. Meanwhile, we are wholly taken up with things present till our nature is changed by grace." It is the nature of Satan to afflict the mind with so much worry and doubt making it seem as though God is distant or does not exist. He magnifies the errors of our brothers and sisters such that we can regard them as the devil incarnate himself. Sometimes, the devil has played so much music of hatred and bitterness in our minds that venom spews out of an otherwise gentle soul. Satan can magnify your misery so much that he makes you forget the joys of yesterday and the hope for the future.

Many people have ruined their futures because the devil made them believe that they cannot overcome what happened yesterday. I have guarded my heart so jealously that I have not allowed the leftovers of yesterday's pain to linger just for a moment in my mind. I have by the grace of God, fought against the "beasts of Ephesus" of my yesterday's pain and betrayal. I have learned to forgive and do so continuously, and I live a life free of stress and worry. I have seen the power of taking control of my mind and subjecting it to Christ and His will. God has been my anchor and comfort.

Sadly, many Christians claim to forgive but they do not forgive well. In order for us to break the cycle of defeat, we must not only forgive, but we must forgive well. Prophecy never swells from a heart of bitterness and anger. Prophecy never works in the life of one who is bitter or angry. A prophet must never be bitter or angry, even though they may deliver a message with so much fiery anger, indignation and judgment. When a prophet becomes bitter and angry, it ceases to be God. Yet the message of the prophet can come out with so much fury and anger—anger at the sin, not the sinner; anger at the disobedience, not the people.

Prophecy, if well understood and divinely implemented spare not failure or defeat. At the very presence of true prophecy, sin melts and its grip is broken, and consequently, the cycle of defeat is shattered and never to emerge again. Peter reminds us, "We have the prophetic word confirmed, which you do well to heed as a light that shines in a dark place" (2 Pet.1.19). When light appears, darkness has to give way. When the good comes to the city, the evil has to flee away out of the city. When beauty comes, then ugly has no place; just as when the truth comes, no lie can stay. Prophecy is so powerful, yet generation after generation, people treat prophecy with contempt. Paul warned the believers "Do not treat prophecies with contempt but test them all; hold on to what is good, reject every kind of evil" (1 Thess. 5.20-21, NIV). yet humanity often do the opposite and have allowed the cycle of defeat to cage their lives.

God's Word is powerful. It is the word of God that prevails in Matthew 4, during the temptation of Jesus. Satan only bowed down to the word of God. This is what prophecy is— to knowing the mind of God. How can I be in bondage if I know the mind of God? To know God is to know the way out of the cycle of defeat and despair, but it must be to know him well. Paul says, "That I may know Him" (Phil.3.10)—that is, to know Christ well. The God's little devotional book for leaders remarks, the secret of success is to do the common thing uncommonly well." If you believe, believe well. If you have to fight against something, then fight well. If you have to pray about something, make sure you pray well. This is my secret: I never just do things for the sake of doing them. Whatever I choose to do, I will do it well. I will do it in such a way that no one will ever do it again and nobody will do it that well. Life is full of things half-done, and we see it everywhere. Let not your efforts be obscure and whatever you do, whether for man or God, do it heartily, as to the Lord. Your success depends on how well you do things.

The same author wisely wrote "The way to get to the top is to get off your bottom." How can you rise to the top of human achievement or to the top of ministry, unless you get off your bottom and soar with wings like an eagle? Many Christians are not willing to face the truth, yet the Word of God says, "You shall know the truth, and the truth shall make you free" (John 8.32). Many people avoid the truth. Prophecy presents the truth to us and says, "Here is the truth; unless you accept it, you will forever remain in the cycle of defeat." Prophets will tell you, "You see this sin, it will not take you anyway, no matter how trivial it may look in your eyes." They will tell you of the small foxes in your life that wants to spoil the vine of your life that is blooming.

In order for you to succeed in life, you must quickly face the reality, do not avoid the truth, embrace it no matter how painful. A great man is always willing to be little, if necessary, while a foolish man will hold on to their title or crown—even while chopping off their own head.

One has to now wonder: how will they wear the crown? It's the work, not the title, that makes us great.

In modern terms, prophecy is a reality check. It wields so much influence that, even though you may not believe it, its impact in your life will always leave footprints. Though Ahab rejected the prophetic Word from Micaiah, the son of Imlah; the impact of that word has become historical. Though Jezebel sought to kill Elijah, God's prophet, the prophetic message ultimately prevailed. Israel rejected Jesus Christ of Nazareth as the prophesied Messiah, yet the power and the profound truth of the prophetic Word has gone beyond Caiaphas, the high priests, and Pontious Pilate, the governor who thought he had power to condemn or set Jesus Christ free. The prophetic message has lived beyond their lifetime. Prophecy is God's speaking in the now.

What more do I need than for God to speak to me now? If God speaks to me now, I know without a shadow of doubt that no cycle of defeat will remain. Do not be afraid to start; those who started must not be afraid to fail, and those who fail must not be afraid to start again. Here lies the mystery of life: "The man who makes no mistakes usually does not make anything." if you don't make mistakes, you are probably dead and you have been dead all along. When you make mistakes, you are probably living and you are trying to do something. Don't mind the naysayers but believe God and His Word: "A righteous man may fall seven times and rise again" (Prov. 24.16).

Prophecy is to believe that wrong can change to right, that sin can yield to righteousness, and that the cycle of defeat can give way to the cycle of victory and triumph, singing songs of celebration. For the people of Israel, prophecy turned 430 years of gloom and despair into hope and possibilities, for God released His people through the power and the mystery of the prophetic message. You will encounter the power and the anointing of revelation. To believe prophecy, is to give your life a chance to breathe again, against the choking hands of defeat and despair. Prophecy is the seed that fell on good ground, and it will always produce a harvest. Hold on to the Word of God—it is the master key that opens the cage of defeat and despair, releasing you into the future you always dreamt about. You are about to experience the reality of your dreams and aspirations.

Read this book slowly and meditatively; your life will take a turn you never imagined possible. If you want to know how this will happen, then consider reading chapter ten of this book, it is in that chapter that you will discover the mystery and the mastery necessary to live beyond mere human existence.

11

Ancient Wisdom in Dealing with Difficult Battles

We have reached a critical stage in learning and understanding how to break the cycle of defeat. This is a moment to sit back, pause, and seriously reflect on your journey so far. How much have you truly understood? What have you learned in the last nine chapters of this book? Breaking the cycle of defeat is both a strategic and spiritual decision. I have extensively taught that there are serious questions we need to seriously consider if we are to achieve anything meaningful. Life must be lived on purpose and on principle; it must not just be lived just as life.

To address the key issues affecting how your life is going, critical questions are necessary. These questions ought to be asked and attended to with greater detail and analysis. They include the *what, why, who, how,* and *when* questions:

1. The "what" question
2. The "why" question
3. The "how" question
4. The "who" question
5. The "when" question

If you are going to be successful in dismantling the strongholds that Satan has built to cage your life and obstruct the wonderful things God has prepared for you, it is essential to believe in and trust God's promises. God has made an unequivocal promise to you: "For I know the thoughts that I think toward you, says the Lord, thoughts of peace and not of evil, to give you a future and a hope" (Jer 29.11). God's plan for you is very clear and straightforward; it is settled and confirmed.

You need to believe in God's plan for your life and allow Him to fulfil His promise to you. God is not slack or slow concerning His promise to His children. The answers of God are "Yes and Amen" (2 Cor 1:20). What blessed assurance we have in God's word, of the ultimate and definitive plan of God for His beloved children.

You are part of God's plan—not because of anything you have done or can do, but because of what Christ has freely offered by dying on the cross and paying the ultimate price to redeem your life. Whether or not you believe God's Word for you, it remains sure, true, and settled. Therefore, no matter what you are going through right now, as you read this book, remember that God has already provided a way out for you. As scripture affirms, "No temptation has overtaken you except such as is common to man; but God is faithful, who will not allow you to be tempted beyond what you are able, but with the temptation will also make the way of escape" (1 Cor 10.13).

God in his extraordinary knowledge and wisdom has provided an answer for you. Before you enter into a situation or storm that seems to be shaking you, I want to assure you that God has already provided a way out for you. This truth is what the devil does not want you to know; he wants you to believe that God has abandoned you and left you alone. But, beloved, I want you to know that God is with you. His promises are clear and true: "Many are the afflictions of the righteous, but the Lord delivers him out of them all" (Ps 34.19). What a grand promise we have from the Lord! Do you believe it? Are you laying hold of it as a weapon to fight the battle and break the cycle of defeat?

THE SECRET OF BREAKING THE CYCLE OF DEFEAT | 111

In every battle you engage in, you need tools with which you can use to fight. What are your spiritual tools? What are your physical tools by which you can wage war, the war against the vicious cycle of defeat? No soldier will ever go to battle without first assembling the weapons, by which he will fight the battle with. You cannot enter into battle until you have clearly identified and defined what tools you need to use to fight against the cycle of defeat successfully. How you fight the battle is also determined by what kind of tools you have to fight the battle with.

The questions I have formulated above—what I call strategic tools—are important in fighting against the cycle of defeat. Defining what we are doing in the battle is extremely important. The next key element is asking why we are engaging in the battle, followed by how the battle will be fought. We then define who are the actors or soldiers in the battle and lastly, when do we plan to fight the battle.

These questions are not just questions, they are indeed strategic questions. We are at a spiritual level of maturity where we clearly understand that battles should not be fought for the sake of fighting; rather, they should be fought with a strategic mindset. Unless you know the outcome of the battle, why would you bother to enter into it? If I were a boxer, I would not enter into the boxing ring unless I had carefully considered the possibilities and the outcomes of the battle.

Paul captures this principle, saying, "When I was a child, I spoke as a child, I understood as a child, I thought as a child; but when I became a man, I put away childish things" (1 Cor 13.11). So, when you were a child, you acted like a child but when you have become a grown man, you act differently and strategically. Maturity should be reflected in the way you define what is important in the battle so that you only focus on what truly matters. You need spiritual sobriety and understanding as you frame the matrix of your battle. You need to run in such a way that you win the crown and you cannot risk just fighting, but you fight to win the battle.

In this chapter, I will show you, without a shadow of doubt, how you can do this. The secrets and principles are revolutionary and determinant. God is the God of victory, and wherever God is involved, victory and success are guaranteed. Many Christians talk about God but they do not truly know God. When you intimately know God, you will understand that in His grand design of things, there is no room for failure or defeat. The aroma of victory scents every battle that God is commanding. The secret is to allow God to occupy and be at His rightful place in your life.

You may wonder why God requires your permission to act in your life, thinking perhaps that He could simply position Himself in His rightful place. However, God is a God of order and protocol. Everything God has designed; it has been given a certain spiritual protocol and order; In order for it to function the way God designed it to function. God is not willing to violate the set spiritual protocol because it is not in his nature and character to do so. Therefore, in fighting against the cycle of defeat, one has to have the spiritual matrix together.

The spiritual formulation of the spiritual journey and the spiritual nuances that would be observed and followed is a very important aspect of the preparation of the battle. Sadly, I am often surprised that Christians whom I expect to be spiritually alert and sound, the majority are spiritually dumb and blind. They often fall into the trap of the devil and have become Satan's trophy in his grand demonic design. But do not worry; I am about to help you reconfigure your mindset and relaunch your life, especially your spiritual life, so that you can fight and fight successfully. I have spent a lot of years privately studying the spiritual world, what it is and how it functions and how we can harness it for the betterment of humanity.

The truth is, every battle is won in the spirit first. You will not be able to win a battle in the physical realm unless the spiritual atmosphere around it has been ordered to give way and allow you leverage. As Proverbs 4.7 states, "Wisdom is the principal thing; therefore,

THE SECRET OF BREAKING THE CYCLE OF DEFEAT | 113

get wisdom. And in all your getting, get understanding." Solomon the greatest wise man who ever lived said, you need wisdom but that wisdom must be craftily handled in such a way that it must give you understanding. This is the crux of the matter: You need spiritual understanding of the battle and why Satan has pitched the battle against you and what you can do so that he will never win the battle. It takes discipline and faith and a higher level of spiritual understanding in order for you to do so.

How much time have you invested in understanding the spiritual battle you are about to fight? How well do you spiritually articulate the battle, and how well do you command the battle? I want you to know that there are two times you are likely to be extremely vulnerable to the devil and to the battle you are fighting: first, when you do not know the battle, you are fighting and when you do not know your enemy and his tactics. The second point is when you seem to know everything about your enemy, such that you seem overconfident, and you undermine your enemy, causing you to enter into the realm of spiritual carelessness. Have you seen people who have lost the battle because they overrate themselves and underestimate the enemy, that they now fight carelessly and allow loopholes and spiritual gaps that would cause them to lose the battle.

Take the Titanic, though a gigantic ship built with the greatest expertise and craftsmanship, was sunk by small holes. Solomon warns us, "Catch us the foxes, the little foxes that spoil the vines, for our vines have tender grapes" (Song of Sol. 2.15). Similarly, I always say, be careful of the small holes in your character, it is the tiny and seemingly harmless holes that will eventually sink your life and destiny and otherwise great destiny. There is no room for spiritual complacency and foolishness. Many people expose themselves to unnecessary risk because of their lack of spiritual understanding. I want you to get it right here. It's important and don't miss it because the success of your life depends on it.

Paul urged the Corinthians to become spiritually minded, saying, "But the natural man does not receive the things of the Spirit of God, for they are foolishness to him; nor can he know them, because they are spiritually discerned. But he who is spiritual judges all things, yet he himself is rightly judged by no one. For 'who has known the mind of the Lord that he may instruct Him?' But we have the mind of Christ" (1 Cor 2.14-16). Unless you are spiritually minded, you will not be able to build that spiritual understanding that is required to help you frame your spiritual battle and fight it.

In this chapter, I will endeavour to show you your way out, but you must seriously pay attention to what you are reading. Renew your mind and reposition yourself to allow you to see the way out. There are many cycles of defeat in everyone's life, and the impact of each cycle is determined by how a person is handling that aspect of their life. However, the spiritual principles that underpin the bases of the fight are universal, and ought to be slightly tweaked to fight the aspect of your life you are addressing. Someone may be fighting the cycle of defeat in their finances, someone in their health, another in their marital life, yet another in their spiritual life.

Let's focus and see what are the important principles we must follow. In every battle, it's important to understand who your adversary is, why he is fighting you, how does he fight and what are his vulnerable points. The Word of God tells you that your adversary, your arch enemy is the devil—Lucifer himself. He is a creature of rebellion, pride and spite. He hates everything that resembles God and anyone who attempts to live a life pleasing to God, he will mark and wage a relentless battle, to try and manipulate and destroy. Jesus warns that the enemy comes "to steal, and to kill, and to destroy," but He also promises, "I have come that they may have life, and that they may have it more abundantly" (John 10:10). God's strategy is futuristic, He knows the future and hold it in the palm of His hands. You are not an accident, and God is aware of your battle even before they begin.

Every battle requires the help of prayer, faith and action. You cannot win the battle against Satan unless you have summoned yourself to a life of devoted and disciplined prayer. Prayer changes everything; it is the most important tool one must use to dismantle the strongholds of the enemy and defeat him. But it is not mere prayer, ritual prayer or even lukewarm prayer. It is the fervent prayer of a righteous man that "avails much" (Jas 5.16). Prayer wields so much power and influence, and it is a mighty weapon that causes Satan to bow down before a righteous, fearless Christian. If you resist him in prayer, he will flee from you; but it is prayer accompanied by faith, real and unyielding stubborn faith in the word of God. It is faith to believe God and his promises. Remember, God will never promise and not do, but it is faith accompanied by corresponding action. Faith without works is dead (Jas 2.26); faith without action is no faith at all. Those who believe must act on their faith.

You now have the best tools and the best advice. Use it and you will see Satan's cycle of defeat broken over your destiny. I can assure you; your life will not be the same. Implement what you have learned, set the spiritual atmosphere in your life right and everything will come together.

There are certain things that are worth noting; understand this and apply it to your life. Understanding, especially spiritual understanding is the lethal weapon one can use against the devices of Satan. Michael Brown writes, "When Christ is present, evil cannot remain. When Jesus is with us, so is the Trinity. When the Trinity is with us, our very Creator is at hand. And God is infinitely more powerful than Lucifer and all the fallen angels combined." The presence of Jesus Christ, the son of God, in the midst of the battle changes everything. Storms may arise but His presence stills the storm of life. Is Jesus' present in your life? What position have you given him? Christ is the commander of the battle and as Michael Brown writes, "The time has come to take the lessons we have learned and employ them for personal development. The time has come to join Christ's work in a more profound manner."

You have learned and have come to understand many things now. Armed with this knowledge, it's time to stand up, dust yourself, reset your mind, and make up your mind that you are going to stand up against the cycle of defeat that Satan has built to cage your life. Stand up and tell yourself that you are not going to sit and complain, but that you are going to do something about it. Stop procrastinating, stand up and start the fight; unless you start, nothing happens. The enemy often intimidates us and challenges us; he dares us so he can paralyze us with fear. Fear is not your portion and you must never allow fear to take hold of your life. Take hold of fear and confront fear right in the eye, declaring that you have been given power over it and it will not torment your life and destiny.

Make the first step, and then take another step, and another and soon your life is moving to another realm. Remember, you can "do all things through Christ who strengthens [you]" (Phil 4.13). Stand up and get up and fight for your destiny.

Do not underestimate the power of a mind made-up. You are doing the right thing. "What then shall we say to these things? If God is for us, who can be against us?" (Rom 8.31). In all situations, you are more than a conqueror through Jesus Christ.

In conclusion of this chapter, I want to offer you some advice. Many people are in bondage today because they fail to understand certain principles of life. Never trust the words that are spoken by a person in need, anyone who is in need has the capacity to transform themselves into an Angel of light. It's what people say to you when they are not in need that shows truly who they are to you. It's what a person says to you when they have no need of anything from you, that you should take to heart, and is genuine and sincere. People can say they respect you and value you when they need something. Do they still value you, when their need is met? Do they respect you when they seem to have no need from you.? Watch out for these things in life and you will never be disappointed, or you will not disappoint anyone. Life has a tendency to present to us what it is not. Satan once tempted Jesus by presenting what is not. Are you being tempted by what is not? Be careful if you want to break the cycle of defeat. Trust no one, even yourself, only trust God and you will live in the comfort of His faithfulness. Now step out, your life and destiny are waiting for you. Use the tools you have learned to navigate your journey, and if you are careful, you will reach your destination.

12

The Denouement

It has been a remarkable journey—one that mirrors the realities of your own life. By reading this book to the end, you have, perhaps without realizing it, or necessarily thinking about it, demonstrated the desire and persistence required of someone who wants to break the cycle of defeat and open a new chapter in their life.

Nelson Mandela once remarked, "It always seems impossible until it is done." Indeed, many things in life appear impossible and undoable until we take that first step of faith and start breaking down the mountains before us into small, manageable tasks. Mountains are mountains, and big in our perception. The reality we create in our minds can either make our enemy invincible or visible. It is our mindset that creates perception, and perception, in turn, creates the reality we live by.

Henry Ford rightly observed, "If you think you can, you can; and if you think you can't, you can't." Your mindset is the greatest weapon in your arsenal and, if mismanaged, the most lethal poison the enemy can use to fight you. Your mind needs to be managed well and be set right. Paul reminds us, "Set your mind on things above, not on things on the earth" (Col. 3.2).

Your mind will create a set focus, and that set focus will give you leverage, power and anointing to fight your battle against the cycle of defeat. Personally, I am deeply convinced of the importance of regularly resetting my mind. Satan relentlessly attacks us, and his targets more often is our mind. He makes us think things a certain way, magnifies and exaggerates what we are going through and distorts reality in an attempt to make us doubt the word of God, and doubt the sincerity and the bonafides of others. He casts a cloud of doubt and unbelief and sometimes a cloud of confusion, that weakens and clouds our judgment.

Satan is a schemer, a distorter of truth, and an author of confusion, a liar and a manipulator. He is consistently plotting and plotting against those whom God has lived and made a huge sacrifice. Peter instructs us to "be sober, be vigilant; because your adversary the devil walks about like a roaring lion, seeking whom he may devour" (1 Pet. 5.8).

Sobriety—a state of serenity and a calm mind—is key to guarding against Satan's schemes. Satan often manipulates information through our minds, pushing us to see only a limited perception, convincing us that what he shows us is the whole truth. He does not want us to pause, reflect, or see the complete picture. He seeks to blind us to the opportunities and possibilities God has placed before us. Satan, the archenemy of reason, works tirelessly to block meaningful reflection and dialogue. Yet God invites us to "Come now, and let us reason together, though your sins are like scarlet, they shall be as white as snow" (Isa. 1.18).

Yet, Satan, the master deceptor, will not give you a chance to reason and dialogue. He captures us in the maze of emotions, and I mean highly volatile emotions. Every time when we must pause, reflect and reason, allowing us to reset our position, Satan provokes and invokes a barrage of toxic emotions that result in highly charged and destructive conversations. We often find ourselves quarrelling and angry with those whom we love, and angry and bitter with those whom we must find peace and common ground. All this is the work of the devil.

Sadly, many Christians have not fully mastered Satan's *modus operandi*—his method of operation. We claim to know the devil and understand his strategies, but our day-to-day lives reflect completely the opposite and clearly shows that we do not truly understand his *modus operandi*. It is a tragedy and a double jeopardy of gigantic proportion. Our world seems to be gliding into a Cliff of spiritual disaster and ruin. Unless we reset our mindsets, relaunch our approach to life, and understand that we have an enemy, the devil, Lucifer, who sometimes transforms himself as an Angel of light, we leave ourselves vulnerable to his schemes.

Satan's ability to deceitfully masquerade as an angel of light, despite being the utter darkness we must hate and fight vigorously, is the reason he seems to catch and trap unalert and casual, careless Christians.

Many Christians are not truly sober, spiritually alert or clearheaded. The majority of God's children are afflicted by a high voltage of fleshly emotions and are bereft of spiritual understanding and mental sobriety. As a result, Satan often makes their life a trophy in his kingdom. Unless we learn how to disable Satan's tactics and strategies, our life is left in the whim and vicissitudes of Satan.

In this final chapter of an otherwise very important book, crafted and written with divine mastery, I would like to share some profound truths—deep secrets that will awaken your spirit and invigorate your inner man; empowering you to rise up and pitch up your spiritual battle, fight the fight of faith and fight victoriously.

To achieve victory in the spiritual battle, we need wisdom and understanding. As Solomon declares in Proverbs 4.7-9, "Wisdom is the principal thing; therefore get wisdom. And in all your getting, get understanding. Exalt her, and she will promote you; she will bring you honour, when you embrace her. She will place on your head an ornament of grace; a crown of glory she will deliver to you." Solomon further emphasizes in Proverbs 24.3-4, "Through wisdom a house is built, and by understanding it is established; by knowledge the rooms are filled with all precious and pleasant riches." These scriptures illuminate how wisdom, which gives birth to understanding, is a key spiritual principle that must be harnessed and applied to change the condition of our life.

Satan also uses fear as a weapon. Fear is paralyzing and destructive, a trap as described in Proverbs 29.25, which states, "The fear of man brings a snare, but whoever trusts in the Lord shall be safe." Fear must be avoided—not by arrogance, but through humility and meekness. Fear is often nothing more than **F.E.A.R.—False Evidence Appearing Real**. Satan uses what we fear to appear to us as if it is real. It is Satan's strategy, but the reality is this, what Satan is telling you is a lie. It is a terrible lie that he has crafted and concocted in order to cage you and suffocate your destiny.

You may say to me, "You are writing as if there is no hope against this creature called Satan." The opposite is true! The reason I am writing to you is that I know you have "an anointing from the Holy One, and you know all things" (1 John 2.20). God has anointed you to destroy the works of the devil. However, you cannot defeat an enemy whom you do not know or whose modus operandi you do not understand. I am drawing from my spiritual knowledge and understanding to uncover and expose your enemy, revealing his schemes so that you can unmask his deceit and stand firm. Satan seeks to tempt and lure you into fighting the wrong battles—battles against flesh and blood—while neglecting the real battle, which is the fight against Satan himself.

Paul warns us in Ephesians 6.12, "For we do not wrestle against flesh and blood, but against principalities, against powers, against the rulers of the darkness of this age, against spiritual hosts of wickedness in the heavenly places." We battle against Satan's spiritual entities and cohorts that he uses to operate for himself, so that he can capture and destroy the believer. Satan's agenda is outlined by Christ in John 10:10: "The thief does not come except to steal, and to kill, and to destroy." But glory to God in the highest, for He has given us His Son, Jesus Christ, as our advocate and sacrifice for sins. Jesus Christ is our intercessor, interceding on our behalf day and night, and through His perfect sacrifice and atonement for our sins, we are able to boldly approach the throne of grace to find mercy and favour in times of need (Heb. 4.16).

Christ came to give us life and life abundantly. As 1 John 3.8 declares, "For this purpose the Son of God was manifested, that He might destroy the works of the devil," including the cycle of defeat and failure. It is unto Christ we look and obtain our complete and total victory. It is in Christ Jesus, and through our relationship with God, that we obtain the measure of the anointing and power necessary for us to fight and break the cycle of defeat.

Humanity often overlooks and is missing the supernatural arsenal found in the divine person of Christ. True victory lies in His kingship and lordship over our lives, and knowing and having a deeper, intimate and abiding relationship with Him. In our deep and sincere walk and fellowship with Christ, the reality of true life is revealed and granted by God the father. In looking unto Christ, the Balm of Gilead, we encounter the great Physician and the mystery of our victory.

We have not taken our relationship with Christ to the spiritual level that God requires of us. The day we sincerely look unto Jesus Christ, the author and perfector of our faith, we will see what real faith does and what mighty works real faith wroughts (Heb.12.2). A real, true and genuine encounter with Christ is necessary and is a prerequisite of a successful Christian life.

When we allow Him to have a genuine space in our hearts and make Him Lord over our lives—not because He is weak and needs our permission, but because He desires our willing obedience not by force—it is then that transformation begins. Christ is love, and he persuades us by love and not by force. He does not use His power and authority as man uses their power and authority.

Christ is the redemption God has offered us against every challenge and storm we may face in this life. Christ is the ultimate power, the power of all powers. In Him, we have complete and total victory over Satan and his devices.

I dare you to believe Christ and believe in what He has accomplished for you already. That is where your redemption starts, and from this place of faith, every cycle of defeat will be broken, and victory will become your testimony. I want you to be encouraged at this point in your life. There are great possibilities and opportunities ahead, despite the darkness and gloom that seems to threaten your future and destiny. God, through His mighty and wondrous Son, Jesus Christ, is able to deliver us from every battle we face. Therefore, you are not fighting for victory—you are fighting from the vantage point of victory. You are therefore fighting from the vantage point of victory, so be confident. This is the victory Christ has offered us, our faith.

www.ingramcontent.com/pod-product-compliance
Lightning Source LLC
Chambersburg PA
CBHW050435010526
44118CB00013B/1543